S0-FIY-603

PROBLEMS OF INDIAN HISTORIOGRAPHY

PROBLEMS OF INDIAN HISTORIOGRAPHY

Edited by

DEVAHUTI

D.K. PUBLICATIONS
29/9, Nangia Park, Shakti Nagar,
DELHI-110007.

First Published, 1979

Rs. 50 $ 10

Published by :

D.K. PUBLICATIONS
29/9, Nangia Park,
Shakti Nagar,
Delhi-110007.

Distributed by :

D.K. PUBLISHERS' DISTRIBUTORS
1, Ansari Road, Daryaganj,
New Delhi-110002
Phone : 274819

Printed by :

HANS RAJ GUPTA & SONS
Anand Parbat, New Delhi

PRIME MINISTER

New Delhi
March 3, 1978

MESSAGE

History has been the record of events which have influenced the pace of civilisation and growth of culture and the consequent emergence of social orders which have been hindered by conflicts or enriched by cooperation between ethnic, religious and linquistic groups over the centuries.

The spiritual foundation of our culture has sustained our endeavour for the improvement in the quality of man and of the democratic institutions through which he seeks to organise social, economic and political life of the community. It should, therefore, be the task of historians to so interpret achievements and failures of struggles undertaken by individuals with the help and support of large masses of people that the need for perseverance in the continuous efforts for the establishment of a just social order does receive an impetus and the forces which seek to wield power for its own sake are subdued. The aim of all human endeavour is in the last analysis the achievement of happiness and peace so that man lives in harmony with himself and with the society.

I am glad that a Conference is being organised in New Delhi by the Indian History and Culture Society and I send my best wishes to it for all success in its deliberations.

Morarji Desai

CONTENTS

Approaches to Indian History

Polity

LIST OF CONTRIBUTORS

Awasthi, A.B.L.
University of Sagaur, Sagar

Awasthi, D.
Ravishankar Shukla University, Raipur

Chakravarti, Uma
Delhi University, Delhi

Chunder, P.C.
Education Minister, New Delhi

Chandra, Pratap
University of Sagaur, Sagar

Chandra, Sudhir,
Aligarh Muslim University, Aligarh

Dixit, Prabha,
Delhi University, Delhi

Jamindar, Rasesh,
Delhi University, Delhi

Kenny, L.B.
Bombay University, Bombay

Misra, Panchanand
Bhagalpur University, Bhagalpur

Misra, R.N.
Jiwaji University, Gwalior

Pande, G.C.
University of Allahabad, Allahabad

Pandey, V.C.
Punjab University, Chandigarh

Puri, B.N.
Lucknow University, Lucknow

Shah K.J.
Karnataka University, Dharwar

Sharma, Krishna
Delhi University, Delhi

Shastri, Ajaya Mitra,
Nagpur University, Nagpur

Singhal, D.P.
Queensland University, Canberra

Sinha, B.P.
Patna University, Patna

Soundara Rajan, K.V.
Archaeological Survey of India, New Delhi
Srivastava, Balram
Banaras Hindu University, Varanasi
Thakur, Vijay Kumar
Patna University, Patna
Tiwari, A.R.G.
Sardar Patel University, Vallabhavidya Nagar
Vajpeyi, Raghavendra
Delhi University, Delhi
Vohra, Ashok
Delhi University, Delhi

PREFACE

HISTORY AND CULTURE encompass a very large area of intellectual activity to include multiple genres of man's response to objects, events, and ideas of which he is at the same time creator, observer and recipient. These genres range from the critically controlled to the imaginative and cognitive. The widening base of education in India—populous, developing, and with a premium on learning in its value system—is leading to a gradual increase in the numbers of those who derive at least their livelihood, if not also moral sustenance, from intellectual activity.

The thoughts and ideas, written and unwritten, produced by this activity, unless regularly exposed to sympathetic and critical evaluation by its holders, both at an intimate-group level and at a wider community and mass media level, face the dangers of inbreeding. There are not so many forums promoting such discussion that one more is too many.

The Indian History and Culture Society has been formed at a time when it has become necessary to ask some basic questions about the study and writing of history in our country. A forum is needed for a dialogue among like-minded as well as contending historians so that a consensus can be reached, no doubt to give rise to conflict and then a further consensus, in a continuing process.

Not only is interaction needed among historians themselves, between them and other social scientists, but also between them and those who make history—the artists, literary writers and philosophers. For it is the activity of these latter which culminates in a norm of collective action and becomes an integral part of concrete history. They are as much the makers of history as the agents of change, both in the sense of evolution and in the sense of permutation and innovation, as are the mechanisms of production and distribution during any age. Integrated history, therefore, is involved with the arts, humanities and social sciences.

For the study of Indian history in general, we are very much in need of Indian frameworks of reference because the general becomes intelligible only through the specific, the universal through the unique. Abstractions are intimately connected with actualities and must flow from them. Moreover, one view of actuality may differ from another in time and space and lead to a different set of abstractions, even in the matter of universal institutions. Thus, not only would the medieval European approach to family and kingship be found to be different from the modern European, but the latter would be unlike the modern American, Chinese or Indian. While different historical approaches are valid for their own time and place, they will ring true to us, if they do, in part or in whole, or not at all, only if we comprehend them in terms of our own reality and our own past experience. We have to be our own 'messiahs', to feel, to understand, to interpret our own history, and to appreciate the validity or otherwise of the 'revelations' of others, of their frames of reference in other words, in our context of time and place.

To comprehend history, we have to keep on observing the remains and reading our sources till we are able to see those objects in use and those people in action. The essential matter of history is not what happened, but what people thought and said about it. The essential matter of Indian history is what the Indian people, ordinary or special, thought and said about events and ideas. It is that self-definition which represents the Indian feel for, attitude towards, and use of history even if it be the rejection of history as real, *i.e.*, of ultimate significance, and therefore its transmutation into myths and symbols. By understanding the process of how they made history, the philosophers, the kings, the social reformers, the artists, the artisans, the tillers, shall we be able to discern their attitude to history. This will supply us with Indian frameworks, possibly dissimilar to each other owing to factors of space, time and external influences. It may indeed be that some of these are analogous to frameworks worked out by other civilizations. The important thing is that we would have cognised them as Indian assumptions. Comparisons with others would, no doubt, provide us with a more meaningful understanding of Indian frameworks.

To discuss these and related questions, the Indian History and Culture Society organised a seminar in March, 1978 on the theme, *Indian History Writing* for which it proposed the frame-work discussed below.

I. The Problem of Identification

(a) We need to know the past in order to discover our identity. The resultant rootedness has the potential of universality necessary for an objective view of history.

It has so far been common, in fact fashionable, to use comparative and alien frame-works for the study of Indian history causing in the process great harm to the student as well as the subject. We need to form and use Indian frames of reference on the basis of the facts of Indian history. Indeed the different frames will coincide in their interpretation of facts upto a point, but beyond that they would diverge in proportion to the difference in their underlying assumptions.

It must also be noted that it is imperative to possess the tool of language of our sources in order to attain historical empathy.

(b) Every civilization is the result of its own specific circumstances but there are also some common features among civilizations. We have to differentiate and compare civilizations in order to arrive at their unique and uniform features respectively.

A case study of Indian history needs to be made from this point of view by studying the interdependence of various determining processes—the physical, the social, the economic, the political, the aesthetic, the ideational, etc., by treating each in turn, as the most dominant. It may well be that different equations suit different periods, and different regions. For example, when a certain degree of political, economic and social stability has been attained, the ideational and the aesthetic processes are likely to play an important role. It may, thus, be fruitful, to view developments during the Gupta or the early Mughal period from this standpoint and see how much these processes affected the social, political, and economic situations.

(c) In studying the uniform forces at the base of civilizations the following may be borne in mind :

(i) *independent response* of different peoples to determining factors, (ii) influences through *diffusion*, and (iii) each civilization's *response to such influences*.

II. Conflict and Consensus

The urges, both for conflict and consensus, are present in human beings. We need to examine the place of each as the motivating factor in individual action and societal progression.

The spirit of consensus requires concession as far as possible ; that of conflict, resistance as far as possible. Progress, *status quo* and stagnation in society would depend on whether or not consensus is supported by conflict and *vice versa*, in the right spirit, the right measure and at the right time. Thus only a continuing watchful structuring of relationships, say, between government and people, father and son, teacher and student would lead to, at the same time, respect for, and equality with each other. Here the validity or otherwise of individual dissent as in the case of Gautama Buddha—in a general framework of stability may also be considered.

We need to examine, at what time, in which fields, Indian society opted for conflict or consensus; also whether Indian society preferred the framework of consensus within which to favour conflict or *vice versa.*

Preference for activity or equilibrium (change or stability) is determined by physical factors, including geography; ideational process consisting among other things of a cogitative response, in resistance to or in cooperation with the physical factors; structure of society, economic necessities, nature of political authority, etc. To give an example of the latter most : The reaction to the phenomena of activity and equilibrium of a business-class-dominated political authority would be different from that of an intellectual-class-dominated political authority.

The divergent pulls in Indian society, thus, the country's size and physical features, ethnic, linguistic, religious, and cultural diversity, etc., as well as the convergent pulls natural and deliberate, and their mutual interaction may be taken into account in an attempt to discover the reasons behind the motivating factors for conflict or for consensus.

III. Ancient Terms and Modern Connotations

The connotation of terms, specially if they have conceptual content often alters radically with the passage of time. The phenomenon is explicable in terms of the changing historical situation. The confusion becomes worse confounded when the terms are translated in a foreign language. Apart from the problems of language and culture-differentiation, the deliberate prejudices, if any, of the translator further vitiate the situation.

The interpretation of ancient and medieval Indian concepts and institutions, and thus of Indian history in general, has suffered greatly on this account in the last hundred years or so. It is imperative that we try to understand the meaning of such terms in the context of their time and place with the help of original sources. In fact, we should try to give up inadequate English equivalents in order to get a true feel of the meaning of such terms which only comes from using them.

Some such terms are : *Dharma*, *Danda*, *Rashtra*, *Samanta*, *Zamindar*, *Vakil*, etc.

IV. Classification of Periods (Periodization) & Classification of Regions

Indian historiography has seen various illogical classifications with regard to periods and regions.

Emphatic on the diversities and lukewarm on the compositeness of Indian culture, British writers gave the categories North and South India which we continue to foster. They also compartmentalised Indian history into three periods and devised the inconsistent and historically incorrect nomenclature, Hindu, Muslim and British for that purpose. Since then we have renamed the periods as Ancient, Medieval, and Modern after the European model. The terms, once again, are value-laden in their connotation. The whole question needs re-examination. Neither period nor region should be regarded as fixed categories. Their classification should be determined by factors such as the nature of historical enquiry, methodological criteria, a dominant historical situation etc. In this connection, we may also take into consideration the distinction between Past, *i.e.*, Oral Tradition, and History, and the importance of the former in the Indian context.

V. Approaches to Indian History

The various standpoints from which Indian history has been viewed: the imperialist or nationalist *i.e.*, in terms of narrow foreign or native self-interest; communalist or marxist, *i.e.*, in terms of religious or economic factors; genealogical or ethnic, *i.e.*, in terms of dynastic or linguistic domination; insular, through neglect of, or over-emphasis on regions, movements etc; romantic or cynical, *i.e.*, oblivious either of the dark or the bright aspects of a given situation, and so forth.

There is need for a scientific, as well as indivisible, approach to history which would treat facts with respect and not use them to serve causes ; which, moreover, would take into account all the urges of man and all the forces that fashion history, social, political, economic, aesthetic, religious, moral, etc. This should be found possible if there is : (1) amplitude of source materials, (2) right discernment and impartiality in their selection, and (3) a keen analysis leading to a causal relationship of facts on the one hand, and on the other the discovery of their social meaning and cultural significance.

VI. Polity

1. Interpretations of Kautilyan polity :
   a) Social,
   b) Political,
   c) Economic.
2. State *versus* Society
3. Relation between legislative, executive and judicial functions. The inner dynamics of the legislative function.
4. The concept and practice of empire : (a) *Chakravarti* and the *mandala* theory, and (b) Balance between centralisation and regional autonomy.

Some topics elicited greater response than others as evident from the number of contributions to each section. However, audience participation on all topics was keen and extensive. The results of the discussions have been incorporated in the text of the papers wherever possible.

173 delegates, from over 30 universities, colleges and other academic institutions from every part of the country attended the seminar contributing towards their expense. In addition to history a number of other disciplines were represented such as archaeology, political science, sociology, philosophy, creative arts, religion, etc. A multiplicity of views was aimed at by inviting academics with different backgrounds and known for their diverse, often conflicting approaches. The seminar, we believe, succeeded both in attracting scholarship of high order and in gaining the involvement of a number of aspiring academics. This is reflected in the papers assembled. For any qualitative inequality we offer no apology. A sense of participation on the part of many is as important to us as the consummate scholarship of the few. Our concern is as much with honest effort as with achievement.

The Indian History and Culture Society contemplates an active future. For 1979 it has planned two seminars. One, on Bias in Indian Historiography to be held in February 1979 and the other on the Aryan problem later in the year. There is, in fact, a keen need for interchange of ideas on a number of fundamental issues as well as on several important subjects. The Society hopes to provide opportunity for discussion on them through workshops and seminars. We need to identify, for instance, the components of our culture on the basis of which generalisations are made, and to understand, perhaps, the spirit of our tradition which we seek to harmonise with modernity. We also need to deal with specific problems of immediate relevance, such as India's political culture, the role of the intellectual, the rationale of Hindu communalism, the rationale of Muslim communalism, the linguistic ethos and so forth.

The Indian History and Culture Society intends to have a base as wide as permissible under its title, with regard to participants, subjects to be discussed and activities to be carried out. It invites the participation and cooperation of all scholars sympathetic to its aims and ideals.

The Society and the seminar owe so much to so many that it would not be possible to list the names individually. It was the zeal and sense of involvement of every one concerned—workers behind the scene, participants, contributors to papers, chairpersons of all the sessions, discussants, and rapporteurs which made the seminar a success. To thank Dr. S.P. Gupta would be redundant ; without him the Society that organised the seminar would not have been. At the same time Dr. Gupta has the great gift of generating in anything that he initiates its own momentum from within, right from the moment of its inception.

Our appreciation is due to the publishers for bringing out this volume, so neatly and efficiently in record time.

Devahuti

Delhi
Jan. 1979

INTRODUCTORY REMARKS

DEVAHUTI

My respected colleagues and friends :

We are overwhelmed by the response to our new organisation and seminar. Even to those of you who have come here out of sceptical curiosity we are grateful, for you have not prejudged us and are not absent out of apathy, indecisiveness, cowardice or prejudice-some of the curses of our present day intellectual life. You have come to find out more about our organisation and to participate in the seminar.

Among the various reasons why you are here, the most important must surely be that like us you too have been disturbed about questions that are vital to us as intellectuals in general and as historians and social scientists in particular. What is the role of the intellectual in society and what does he take from it; what does and should he give to it? What should be his attitude towards government, any government, irrespective of his own political or moral ideology? What should be the society's and the government's attitude towards the intellectual? What should be the historian's frame of reference — should his purpose be to serve history or to use history for a purpose.

Although the intellectual, by the nature of his pursuit, prefers to plough a lonely furrow, should he not, in the present circumstances try to join a group and form a forum for exchange of views, similar and dissimilar.

With the rapidly growing size of the intellectual community the need was felt for setting up a new society but that alone would not have given us enough incentive to make the effort. The rationale for the setting up of the Indian History and Culture Society lies in providing a forum for what we might term *the third alternative* in the present state of affairs.

Historiography in modern India has been "a kind of permanent civil war" and we thought that we had better do something about it. One group of historians—to include the Imperialists, the Marxists along with a sub-class of pseudo — secularists, and finally the Muslim communalists justify their widely different stands, by denigrating Indian tradition; the other group to include — the nationalists and the Hindu communalists romanticise Indian tradition. But there is a third set of historians who being products of the same milieu — and inheritors, no doubt, of the dominant predilections of the age-political, ideological, and religious are yet struggling to strike a new path — to write objective history with a cruel awareness of the inevitable subjective element in it.

Such historians have suffered the lack of a forum for too long. This is their Society. It is their Society not to the exclusion of the Marxist, the Nationalist or the Muslim or Hindu communalist, because problems are solved by being faced, not by being shelved. However, problems can only be discussed when you have a forum. The old forums that were there, the third alternative intellectuals in general, and historians in particular allowed to be turned into monoliths. The reasons for it lie in a slow erosion of their moral fibre on the one hand, and on the other, their non-fanaticism, a necessary concomitant of inclusivism. Sizable cracks have appeared in the monoliths, whether at the universities, in academic bodies or in the strongholds of mass media. But they would get plugged if they are not widened; if the historians continue to view humanism as a parallel stream with economic determinism rather than buttress one with the other and evolve a new thinking of which the strength will lie in a continuous state of adjustment. The hard realities of life in the country provide the directives for it. The need of the spirit and of the body have to be satisfied simultaneously. It is indeed possible to do so because they do not run counter to each other. The basic and vital difference between the inclusivist and the exclusivist intellectual, and in the history world between the multi-model and the economic-determinist historian lies in confusing one of the means — the economic betterment of man, with the ideal — his total betterment, to include economy, aesthetics and morality.

Friends, there is one among our participants here, Dr. P.C. Chunder, who is present in his twin capacities as an academic and a representative of the government. The baneful effects of partisanship on the part of any government of any country are too well known to historians to be recounted here. While the vicious circle created by such acts has got to be snapped and that cannot be stressed too strongly—to remove the psychosis of fear that still prevails, the major role of government as such remains to create conditions in which diversity can prosper. If the intellectuals, the historians of the third alternative do not want struts, they have to combine moral courage with an extra effort to create, to produce more, and of a quality representative of their values, that will help the government break the vicious circle.

We trust that they will use this forum, the Indian History and Culture Society, for that purpose.

पृष्ठ भूमि

बुजुर्गो, दोस्तो और साथियो, इस पुस्तक के माध्यम से मैं आप सबका हार्दिक स्वागत करता हूं क्यों कि अब आप सबने मिल कर यह तय कर लिया है कि आप अपने लिए एक ऐसे मंच का निर्माण करेंगे जहां आप स्वतन्त्र रूप से अपने विचारों का आदान-प्रदान कर सकें। आज से करीब दो साल पहले मेरे मन में एक विचार आया था : कौटिल्य के अर्थशास्त्र को नए परिपेक्ष में क्यों न देखा जाय। मैं स्वयं पुरातत्व का विद्यार्थी हूं और इस नाते इतिहास के केवल एक स्त्रोत से ही मेरा निकट का परिचय रहा है। इस देश में अनेक विद्वान हैं जिन्हें इतिहास के अन्य स्त्रोतों पर मुझसे कहीं ज्यादा दखल रहा है अतः क्यों न हम सब मिलकर उस पर विचार करें। स्वयं में यह विचार आने पर मैंने उन कुछ विद्वानों से सम्पर्क किया जिन्होंने कौटिल्य पर कुछ ठोस कार्य किया है—प्रो. बिन्देश्वरी प्रसाद सिन्हा, प्रो. प्रताप चन्द्र, प्रो. लल्लन जी गोपाल, आदि। 2 मई 1966 को औरों को भी पत्र लिखे। सबने इसका स्वागत किया मगर साथ ही यह सुझाव भी दिया कि इतिहास के ऐसे और भी अनेक मुद्दे हैं जिन पर हम लोग समय समय पर अपने विचारों की अदला-बदली करना चाहेंगे। वास्तव में इसी समय डा. देवहुति ने 'भारतीय इतिहास लेखन—एक आत्म-परीक्षा', पर एक पूरी योजना ही रख दी। प्रो. गोपाल ने आर्यों पर एक परिचर्चा करने का सुझाव दिया। इस प्रकार से अब तीन विषय हमारे सामने आ गए। क्योंकि कार्य बढ़ने का डर लगने लगा अतः मैंने दिल्ली के कुछ एक अन्य महानुभावों से भी सम्पर्क स्थापित किया। डा. बी. आर. ग्रोवर, श्री बाल कृष्ण थापड़, श्री मुनीश चन्द्र जोशी, श्री के. एस. रामचन्द्रन, आदि सभी ने इस कार्य में अपना पूरा योगदान देने का वचन दिया। इन सभी ने जोरदार तरीके से यह कहा कि अच्छा हो अगर हम लोग मिलकर शीघ्र ही एक नए छोटे मंच का विधिवत निर्माण कर लें जिसके माध्यम से समय समय पर लोगों को हम औपचारिक रूप से बुला सकें और जिसे आवश्यकतानुसार वित्तीय सहायता लेने का अधिकार भी प्राप्त हो। 28 मई 1966 को एक अस्थायी कार्यकारिणी का गठन भी हो

गया। लेकिन इस सब के दौरान मैंने लोगों से यह कहा कि इस कार्य में एक ही संदेह मुझे लग रहा है और वह यह है कि इंडियन हिस्ट्री कांग्रेस के अपने मित्र कहीं इस गलतफहमी के शिकार न हो जाँय कि यह मंच उनके विरोध में खड़ा किया गया है। इसके बारे में जो मुझे सभी छोटे बड़े से उत्तर मिला वह कुछ यों था : आजकल हिस्ट्री कांग्रेस एक मेला हो गया है। सेशन्स में इतने थोड़े लोग होते हैं जब कि उद्घाटन में भीड़ होती है कि अक्सर लोगों से पूछना पड़ता है 'क्या जब में अपना पेपर पढ़ रहा होऊंगा उस समय आप उपस्थित रहने की कृपा करेंगे ?' हमारा मंच तो उससे कहीं ज्यादा छोटा होगा जहाँ हम आमने-सामने बैठ कर ज्यादा इन्टीमेट तरीके से बातचीत कर सकेंगे। हमारा उद्देश्य बहुत सीरियस काम करने का है। एक बात और : हिस्ट्री कांग्रेस केवल इतिहासकारों की जमायत है जब कि हमारा उद्देश्य उससे अधिक व्यापक होगा—इसमें भारतीय संस्कृति के और पहलू भी होंगे, जैसे दर्शन शास्त्र, भारतीय भाषायें, कला, कौशल, नृत्य, वादन, सभी। हमारे कार्य का स्कोप बहुत विस्तृत होगा। हमारा कैनवास बहुत बड़ा है। इस लिए कोई डुप्लीकेशन नहीं है भले ही कुछ ओवरलैपिंग हो। मैं स्वयं जीवन में किसी भी हिस्ट्री काँग्रेस के सम्मेलन में गया नहीं। उसका सदस्य ही नही बना। अतः व्यक्तिगत रूप से उसके तौर तरीके से अनभिज्ञ हूं। स्वयं ट्रेडीशनलिस्ट किस्म का हिस्ट्रोरियन अपने को मानता भी नहीं ; हूं भी नहीं। आर्ट, आर्कलॉजी में अपने को मैंने डुबा रखा है जिसे भारत के बहुत सारे इतिहासकार इतिहास की श्रेणी में गिनते ही नहीं, भले ही आर्कलाजी के उगते सूरज में अपने पंख फड़फड़ाने की अनाधिकार चेष्टा वे स्वयं क्यों न कर रहे हों। जो भी हो, मेरा व्यक्तिगत मतभेद हिस्ट्री कांग्रेस के किसी भी कार्यकर्ता से कभी भी नहीं रहा क्योंकि मेरा उनसे कभी भी लेना-देना नहीं रहा। इसलिए उस संस्था का विभाजन करके किसी नई संस्था को उसके विरोध में खड़ा करने का प्रश्न मेरे मन में भी कभी उठा ही नहीं। यह बात सितम्बर मास की है जब हमारा परामर्श ज़ोर पर चल रहा था। नवम्बर की पहली तारीख को एक ड्राफ्ट कांस्टीट्यूशन तैयार हो गया। वह आप लोगों को भेज दिया गया था।

मगर कुछ समय बाद ही एक छोटी सी घटना और घट गई जिसका लाभ उठाकर दिल्ली के प्रमुख समाचार पत्रों ने हमारे सामने एक संदेहात्मक स्थिति पैदा कर दी। वह घटना यूं थी । दिसम्बर की 12 तारीख को इंडिया इन्टरनेशनल सेंटर में एक पैनेल डिस्कशन आयोजित हुआ जिसके विषय में हिस्ट्री टेक्स्ट बुक्स की कान्ट्रोवर्सी थी। आयोजकों ने किस उद्देश्य से मुझ जैसे पुरातत्व के एक छोटे से विद्यार्थी को उस ऊंचे मंच पर

बुलाया जिसका संचालन निहार बाबू जैसे चोटी के इतिहासकार करने वाले थे, मैं आज तक नहीं समझ पाया । अख्बारों के माध्यम से पिछले तीन मास से बहुत कुछ कहा-सुना जा रहा था। मैंने कभी भी किसी भी रूप में उसमें भाग नहीं लिया था । लगभग 15 दिन पहले म्यूजियम में आए निहार बाबू से मैंने पूछा भी कि मुझे क्यों घसीटा जा रहा है एक उस परिसंवाद में जिससे मुझे कोई खास लेना-देना नहीं । क्या मैं आऊं ? उन्होने भी वही कहा कि उन्हें कुछ भी मालूम नहीं लेकिन, 'यदि आयोजकों ने बुला ही लिया है तुम्हें तो पुरातत्व के बारे में तुम अपना मत जरूर दे सकते हो । वैसे मुझे इस सारे बहस में अपनी कोई रुचि नहीं ।'

कला और पुरातत्व पर निहार बाबू से मैंने बहुत कुछ सीखा है यद्यपि कि मैं कभी भी उनका विधिवत विद्यार्थी नहीं रहा । मुझे उनका बहुत आदर रहा है और उन्होने हमेशा मुझे अपना स्नेह दिया है । घंटों म्यूजियम में और घर पर मेरी उनसे अनेक विषयों पर चर्चा हुई है । अर्बानाइजेशन से लेकर मौर्य, शुंग और कुषाण कला तक पर । मुझे लगा कि वे स्वयं भी चाहते हैं कि मैं निर्भीक रूप से इन पुस्तकों के पुरातत्व के अंशों पर अपना विचार दूं । मैंने इसे उनकी आज्ञा समझी । तब मैंने प्रो. राम शरण शर्मा जी की ग्यारहवीं कक्षा की प्राचीन इतिहास की पुस्तक खरीदी और केवल उन अध्यायों को पढ़ा जो नितांत पुरातत्व से सम्बन्धित थे । सम्मेलन हुआ और जोरदार हुआ । ऐतिहासिक हुआ । भरा हुआ हाल था । जो कुछ गलतियाँ थी उस पुस्तक में मैंने उन्हें मौखिक और लिखित रूप में सबके सामने रखा । शायद निहार बाबू को भी इन गलतियों का जरा भी आभास नहीं था । मैंने वहीं अपने हर कथन पर कहा है कि यदि मैं गलत होऊँ तो वहीं उसी समय वे बतायें । किन्तु वे चुपचाप सुनते रहे, क्या कहते । बाद में उन्होंने मुझसे कहा, "गुप्ता, सचमुच मुझे बड़ा खेद है कि इस छोटी सी पुस्तक में इतनी फैक्चुल मिस्टेक्स हैं । मुझे इसका कोई ज्ञान नहीं था । लेकिन मुझे डर है कि अखबार वाले इसी को उछालेंगे जबकि असली मुद्दा कुछ और ही था आज की बातचीत का—सरकारी हस्तक्षेप का मुद्दा था ।" मैं क्या उत्तर देता । मैंने सिर्फ इतना ही कहा, "मैं तो यहां आपसे पूछ कर आया था और मैंने सिर्फ ही उतने ही हिस्से पर अपनी बात कही जितनी पर आपने मुझे इजाजत दी थी ।"

इसके बाद तो उत्तर-प्रतिउत्तर का एक और ही दौर शुरू हो गया जिसे दोहराना मैं अपनी प्रतिष्ठा के विपरीत समझता हूं क्योंकि न चाहते हुए भी जो एक बौद्धिक परिसंवाद मात्र था उसे कुछ लोगों ने राजनैतिक रंग दे डाला । बड़े बूढ़े उम्र की गरिमा भुलाकर लेखनी में गाली-गलौज करने लगे । देश भर में सयापा रचा गया । जनमत संग्रह करने के लिए लोगों को खत लिखे

गए भले ही प्रो० संकालिया जैसे विद्वानों ने उसकी मुझसे भी अधिक कड़ी आलोचना की उन पत्रों के उत्तर में। यही नहीं, जो किसी अर्थ में मेरा व्यक्तिगत प्रश्न था उसे हमारी बन रही नई संस्था से जोड़ दिया मानों यही नई संस्था के जन्म का कारण हो। लोगों ने विभिन्न तिथियों का भी ध्यान नही रखा।

इतना सब बताने का कारण केवल यह है कि कम से कम हमारे सदस्यों के मन में यह भ्रामक बात न रह जाय——इस संस्था के जन्म की कहानी और स्कूलों की पाठय-पुस्तकों की बहस में कही दूर-दराज का भी सम्बन्ध नहीं। वास्तव में इस संस्था के निर्माण में जिनका सबसे अधिक बौद्धिक और आत्मिक सहयोग मुझे मिला वे हैं हमारी जनरल सेक्रेटरी श्रीमती देवहूती जी। अपनी अस्वस्थता में भी उन्होंने घंटों काम किया था और इस सेमीनार की पूरी योजना बनाई थी। उनकी विलक्षण कर्मठता ने हम सबको हमेशा प्रेरित रखा था। उधर प्रो० दामोदार प्रसाद सिंहल जी ने आस्ट्रेलिया में रहते हुए भी जिस आत्मीय भाव से मेरा उत्साह बढ़ाए रखा वह भी उसकी अपनी निजी विशेषता है। प्रो. लल्लन जी गोपाल मेने बचपन के मित्रों में हैं अतः उनका सहयोग तो मैंने साधिकार लिया। प्रो. गोविन्द चन्द्र पाडें प्रकाण्ड पंडित हैं एवं मेरे और डा. गोपाल के प्रयाग विश्वविद्यालय में गुरु रहे है अतः हमारे आग्रह पर इस मंच के संचालन का भार लेना उन्होंने स्वीकार किया। प्रो. बिन्देश्वरी प्रसाद सिन्हा जी ने सदा से ही मुझे बहुत स्नेह दिया है। भारतीय पुरातत्व परिषद के निर्माण में जिस सूझ-बूझ का उन्होंने परिचय दिया था उससे मैं हमेशा से यह मानता आया हूँ कि हर संघर्ष के अवसर पर समन्वय पैदा करने की उनकी एक विलक्षण क्षमता है। अतः इस दौरान मैंने समय-समय पर उनका मार्ग-दर्शन पाया है। प्रो. खलीक अहमद निज़ामी भारत के मध्य-युगीन इतिहास के चोटी के विद्वान हैं। आपने बहुत सारे साथियों के साथ उन्होंने शुरू से ही हर कदम पर मुझे नेक सलाह दी है। प्रो. कृष्णदत्त बाजपेई, प्रो. अजय मिश्र शास्त्री, प्रो. के. वी. रमन, डा. शिवकुमार गोयल, आदि ने इस संस्था के संविधान को बनाने में मेरी सहायया की।

समय समय पर मैंने देश के अन्यान्य विद्वानों को व्यक्तिगत पत्र लिखे और मुझे इस समय उन सभी को अपना आभार प्रगट करने में प्रसन्नता हो रही है जिन्होंने सहर्ष मेरे विचारों को सहमति दी। प्रो. सुब्रहमणयम, प्रो. नरसिंह मूर्ति, प्रो. रेड्डी, प्रो. रवीन्द्रन, प्रो. मेहता, प्रो. राय, प्रो. पुरी, प्रो. शाह, डा. प्रताप चन्द्र, डा. जमीनदार, प्रो. केनी, श्रीमती करमारकर, डा. जेना, डा. नौटियाल, डा. सिंह, डा. पाण्डेय, डा. सहाय, प्रो. छाबड़ा,

प्रो. मेहरा, प्रो. नारायण, प्रो. मिश्र, प्रो. मुकर्जी, प्रो. सेन, डा. सक्सेना, डा. श्रीवास्तव, डा. थप्लियाल, प्रो. दत्त आदि सभी के स्नेह भरे पत्र आज भी मौजूद हैं। हाँ, दो चार उन लोगों के नाकारात्मक खत भी मौजूद हैं जिन्होंने बिना संस्था का परिचय प्राप्त किए आई. सी. एच. आर. की मीटिंग में यह दोषारोपण लगा कर संस्था को धन नहीं लेने दिया कि इसमें उन्हें बुलाया नहीं गया और यह संस्था सबके लिए नहीं है। कुछ ने तो पत्रों के जवाब ही नहीं दिए। मगर हमें विश्वास है हमारे सद्कार्य एक दिन सबको सद्बुद्धि देंगे। वे भी इतिहास की सेवा करना चाहते हैं और हम भी। जो भी हो, इस सभी पत्र-व्यवहार के बीच जो एक बात सबसे अधिक उभर कर आई है उसे में आपके सामने रखना चाहूंगा।

इस संस्था का निर्माण न तो किसी व्यक्ति के विरोध में हुआ है और न किसी संस्था के विरोध में। इतिहास साक्षी है कि सिर्फ विरोध में खड़ा हुआ कोई भी कार्य स्थायी नहीं होता। विरोधों की बचकानी हरकतों से अखबारों की स्याही तो खराब की जा सकती है किसी स्थायी मूल्य को जन्म नहीं दिया जा सकता। यह संस्था विद्वानों की है। विचारों के आदान प्रदान के लिए है। विचारों की स्वतंत्रता के लिए है। इसका न तो राजनीति से कोई सम्बन्ध है और न ही इसे किसी सदस्य के व्यक्तिगत राजनैतिक विचारों का थोपा जाना स्वीकार होगा। संस्था के रूप में हम न तो किसी सरकार की वाह वाही करेंगे, न किसी सरकार की हाय हाय। विभिन्न देशों के इतिहास के पन्ने विद्वानों के खून के छींटों से रंगे पड़े हैं। प्राचीन काल के "यो मे श्रमण सिरो दास्यामि........" से लेकर अर्वाचीन काल तक अन्यान्य देशों में विद्वानों का पर्सीक्यूशन हुआ है। हर बादशाहत ने उसका उपयोग भी किया है और दुरुपयोग भी। हर युग की सरकारों ने कानून का हवाला देकर अपनों को गद्दियां दी हैं और असली पंडित को त्याग और तपस्या का पाठ पढ़ा कर उसकी उपेक्षा की है। अकर्मण्यता और मीडियोक्रैसी चाटुकारिता की चाशनी चढ़ाकर सरकारों के सिर पर बोलती रही है और संस्थाओं के भविष्य को नीचे खींचती रही है। सरकारों ने देश की मेधा को उठाया कम है गिराया ज्यादा है। एक देश के एक मंत्री ने एक बार एक विद्वान के लिए कहा था 'We do not want luminaries in government service' मैं सुन कर हैरान था। उठाने वालों ने तो एकाकी दुंदुभी बजाई है। 'एकला चलो रे,' टैगोर ने कहा था। असली क्राँति के अग्रदूत तो हर देश का कोई रूसो रहा है जिसने बार बार यह दोहराया है कि "मैन इज बार्न फ्री यट एवरीह्वेयर इन चेन्स" Man is born free yet everywhere in chains. उधर भगवान ने जब जब किसी विद्वान को जरा भी सत्ता सौंपी है उसके

साथ उसमें उसने भयंकर अहंकार, ईष्या और द्वेष भी साथ में दे दिया है। सच बात तो यह है कि विद्वान विद्वानों की गोष्ठियों में ही मानसिक रूप से स्वस्थ रह पाता है क्योंकि वहीं हर सेर को सवासेर मिलता है। मगर समय का चक्र बदल रहा है। जागरूकता आ रही हैं। अत: सत्ता की राजनीति से हमें कुछ भी लेना-देना नहीं उससे हम अपने को कोसों दूर रखना चाहते है। हम तो विचारों की खुली बहस में विश्वास करते हैं और हमारे दरवाजे सभी बुद्धजीवियों के लिए खुले हैं। 1978 के सत्र में हर वाद, और विचार-धारा के लोगों ने खुल कर भाग लिया। कोई यह नहीं कह सकता कि उसे जबरियन चुप करा दिया गया। मैं स्पष्ट कर देना चाहता हूं कि हम सामूहिक रूप से न तो किसी 'वाद' विशेष के पोषक ही हैं और न उसके विरोध-कर्ता ही। हमारे लिए तो वही बाग सुन्दर हैं जिसमें तरह तरह के फूल खिले हों, वह बाग बिलकुल बेकार है जिससे सिर्फ एक रंग और एक जाति के फूल हों, चाहे वे लाल गुलाबों के ही क्यों न हों।

भारत का इतिहास एक अत्यन्त विस्तृत समुन्द्र है। मैं उन लोगों को क्या कहूं जो इसे 'वादों', के घेरे में बांधने की चेष्टा करते हैं और उन योरोपियों की नज़रों से भारत के इतिहास को देखना चाहते हैं जिन्होंने सौ साल पहले एशियाई देशों के लोगों को हिकारत की नज़र से देखा था भले ही वे गरीबों की भी तरफदारी क्यों न करते रहे हों। हमसे ज्यादा इस सच्चाई को कौन जानता है कि मनुष्यों का इतिहास न कभी नियमों को कसौटी पर कसा जा सका है, न आज तक उसके लॉज ही कोई ढूंढ़ पाया है, और न किसी 'वाद' विशेष की नकेल से ही वह पूरी तरह से गुज़ारा जा सका है। मनुष्यों का इतिहास व्यक्तियों के मस्तिष्कों की गलयों से गुजरता है और सामूहिकता के चौराहे पर कुछ लमहों के लिए ठहरता है, और फिर व्यक्तियों के मस्तिष्कों की गलियों से गुजरने लगता है। इतिहास के हर मोड़ पर कोई न कोई व्यक्ति रहा है जिसे सामूहिकता ने उतना ही चलाया है जितना सामूहिकता को उसने चलाया है। अतः इतिहास व्यक्ति और सामूहिकता के बीच का एक इन्टरऐक्शन है। इसी में 'इतिहास की परिस्थिति' (हिस्टॉरिकल सिचुएशन) जन्म लेती है। हर देश और हर काल में इस 'ऐतिहासिक परिस्थिति' ने एक नया ही रुप लिया है। इसलिए यह कहना आसान नहीं कि इतिहास में व्यक्ति प्रमुख रहा है या सामूहिकता (समाज) या परिस्थिति——अपनी-अपनी जगह तीनों ही प्रमुख रहे हैं। इस नाटक का कोई एक हीरो नहीं।

मगर इस नाटक को देखने जाने के पहले, मैं अपने उन सब कार्यकर्ताओं को अपनी और आपकी तरफ से हृदय से धन्यवाद देना चाहूँगा जिन्होंने रात-दिन एक करके प्रथम अधिवेशन का आयोजन किया था। श्री भीम सेन सिंह,

proceeds. The cultural world is, as it were, pervaded by a distinctive spirit or self-consciousness which is fashioned by history and subsists by way of tradition, especially educational tradition. Identifying a culture, thus, is not like identifying a natural species on the basis of observation from without. It is rather like the critical determination of the essential form and meaning of a poem or a philosophy, which is impossible without entering into the spirit of what is sought to be determined. The advantage which the historian has over other participants arises not merely from his scientific detachment but from his awareness of a larger context. The discovery of cultural identity thus requires a coordination of two enterprises, *viz.*, delving into a cultural tradition itself and viewing it from within, and viewing it in the larger context of universal history. The historian has to participate in the tradition without necessarily accepting it. He must view it *as if* he belonged to it. Only then will the tradition become accessible and yield its inner meaning and form and yet be objectified sufficiently to be placed within the context of history. The identification of a culture, thus, is possible only through this kind of historical empathy, not through a comparison of cultures assumed to be *given as such*.

From this essential ideality as well as historicity of cultural identity, it follows that there cannot be any universal framework of categories for the study of culture. It has been argued on the other side that if such a universal framework were to be rejected the unity of the discipline studying culture will break down as also the possibility of intercultural scientific collaboration. These objections, however, are superficial. An analogy from the study of languages will clarify the truth. Different languages have different structures and use different sets of sounds. What is more, each language seems to analyse the world of experience differently. All this certainly makes communication from one language to another more difficult than communication within the same language. Nevertheless, it does not make languages wholly opaque to other languages.

Just as descriptive sentences about the natural world are the easiest to translate from one language to another,

श्री मनोज कुमार, श्री इन्दुधर द्विवेदी, श्री रासदयाल पाल और मेरे अभिन्न मित्र डा. आर. पी. तिवारी जी ने क्या कुछ नहीं किया। श्री कुमार ने साइक्लोस्टाइलिंग, आदि के कार्य से मुझे मुक्त कर दिया जबकि श्री ईश्वर चन्द्र मित्तल जी ने एक समय के भोजन की व्यवस्था की। विश्व युवक केन्द्र के मैनेजर श्री अशोक वर्मा और उनके साथियों के भी हम हृदय से आभारी हैं क्योंकि जिस आत्मीय भाव से और कार्य क्षमता से उन्होंने हम सबको रखा और हमारे भोजन की व्यवस्था की वह अद्वितीय था। हम लोग इन सभी कार्यकर्ताओं के हृदय से आभारी हैं।

20 जनवरी 1979
नई दिल्ली

स्वराज्य प्रकाश गुप्ता
(संगठन मंत्री)

THE PROBLEM OF IDENTIFICATION

One

IDENTIFYING INDIAN CULTURE

G.C. PANDE

WHILE THE identity of a natural phenomenon is independent of its human recognition, the same cannot be said of a cultural phenomenon. Water, for example, remained a compound even when it was misidentified as an element for a long time. It cannot, however, be said that the holiness or divinity of the *Ganga* subsists outside of its recognition. The understanding of a natural object is completed by placing its perceptible features within a network of cause and effect. A cultural object, on the other hand, *qua* an item in the cultural world does not necessarily belong to any causal scheme. The holy *Ganga* thus belongs to a symbolic order representing moral and spiritual purification. Even where the causal power of a cultural object belonging to it by virtue of its natural aspect is relevant to its cultural status, the object nevertheless is also imbued with social meaning and cultural significance. In entering the cultural world, a natural object becomes a sign or symbol of meaning and purpose. A tractor, for example, is not merely a material thing but also a form of property, a sign of social status and, in a developing country, a symbol of cultural progress.

Culture and cultural recognition are thus mutually relative. We cannot identify a cultural world without taking into account the matrix of awareness from which it proceeds. The cultural world is, as it were, pervaded by a distinctive spirit or self-consciousness which is fashioned by history and subsists by way of tradition, especially educational tradition. Identifying a culture, thus, is not like identifying a natural species on the basis of observation from without. It is rather like the critical determination of the essential form and meaning of a poem or a philosophy, which is impossible without entering into the spirit of what is sought to be determined. The advantage which the historian has over other participants arises not merely from his scientific detachment but from his awareness of a larger context. The discovery of cultural identity thus requires a coordination of two enterprises, *viz.*, delving into a cultural tradition itself and viewing it from within, and viewing it in the larger context of universal history. The historian has to participate in the tradition without necessarily accepting it. He must view it *as if* he belonged to it. Only then will the tradition become accessible and yield its inner meaning and form and yet be objectified sufficiently to be placed within the context of history. The identification of a culture, thus, is possible only through this kind of historical empathy, not through a comparison of cultures assumed to be *given as such*.

From this essential ideality as well as historicity of cultural identity, it follows that there cannot be any universal framework of categories for the study of culture. It has been argued on the other side that if such a universal framework were to be rejected the unity of the discipline studying culture will break down as also the possibility of intercultural scientific collaboration. These objections, however, are superficial. An analogy from the study of languages will clarify the truth. Different languages have different structures and use different sets of sounds. What is more, each language seems to analyse the world of experience differently. All this certainly makes communication from one language to another more difficult than communication within the same language. Nevertheless, it does not make languages wholly opaque to other languages.

Just as descriptive sentences about the natural world are the easiest to translate from one language to another, positive knowledge including science and technology, represents the most communicable part of a culture. If we were to define as civilization that part of culture which is concerned with ensuring the survival of man through the development of social power, especially in terms of environmental control, we could say that communication is an essential part of the contact between civilizations. The struggle for survival, indeed, tends to force upon every progressive civilization the need to adopt the most advanced science and technology of the age. Civilization in this sense certainly shows a tendency to cross cultural borders and become increasingly universal. Nevertheless, in the great realm of values like religion, morality and art, this is not the case. Encounter at this level may become fruitful if the cultures are alive, but the situation will be that of a dialogue between individuals who remain different.

In all cultures so far the basic determinants of identity have to be sought in their system of values and symbols, the word 'system' being used loosely to cover any kind of congeries or assortment. Religion and social ethics constitute the primary value system while language, ritual and art illustrate the symbolic systems; art, in fact, both realizing as well as symbolizing value. Cultural identity in this sense tends to be circumscribed by the barriers of communication. The Arabs, for example, had no difficulty in learning science from the Greeks and Hindus, but there was an obvious barrier as far as communication in the sphere of religion was concerned. It is easy to multiply such examples. The contact of India with the West since the nineteenth century is itself illustrative of the difference in communication between different levels of culture. In fact, the awareness of Indian culture in the modern sense arose from the encounter. Different approaches to the discovery and exposition of Indian culture arose naturally, and the present crisis of cultural identity in India may itself be traced to the continued effort to distinguish the essential from the inessential in the cultural tradition so that it may be understood as a creative continuation with contemporary relevance rather than as a dead burden on its way to the scrap heap of time.

If we think of culture as characterized by its values and area of communication, it would seem at first sight difficult to discover the unity of Indian culture in any distinctive sense. Since cultures like human beings show generic similarities, it is obvious that if we think of Indian culture with sufficient abstractness we would be universalizing it. On the other hand, in individualizing our characterisation we must not forget that no culture with a continental spread and a long history can be homogeneous or monolithic. Thus the individuality of Indian culture must be so interpreted as not to militate against the universality of human nature and value-seeking. At the same time, the unity of Indian culture has to be interpreted with sufficient catholicity to include the numerous communities, regions and epochs which have historically entered into its making. This search for the cultural identity of India, individual but aspiring after universality, one but inclusive of differences, continuous but developing, is a task which arises from the awareness of India's historic traditions. It should not be confused with the search for national integration at the political level. While it is true that the historical boundaries of Indian culture and civilization have been variable, they could never be identified with the political boundaries of any given age.

Reference was made above to religious and moral values as constituting the fundamental values of culture. From this it would seem that since Indian civilization is obviously multi-religious, we could not really speak of a unified culture in India. This, however, is not the case because the spiritual tradition of India accepts the validity of alternative religious systems, *dharma-samavaya* as the greatest ruler of India expressed it. The confusion would perhaps be removed if we were to substitute the phrase 'religious and moral values' by 'spiritual values'. Traditionally, the mystic or the saint with personal realization has been given the highest respect in India. Seeking spiritual realization, called *sadhana* or *yoga*, has been held to be the highest kind of value-seeking. *Sadhana* implies the dedicated and disinterested performance of one's duties whatever it might be—so that one may move forward towards self-realization, The stories of *Dharmavyadha* and *Tuladhara* illustrate how a hunter or merchant could be engaged in spiritual advancement just as much as a learned Brahmana or ascetic. The legends of Bodhisattva striving after Enlightenment in all stations of life illustrate the same universality of *sadhana* and show that it transcends the distinction of sacred and secular as well as the bounds of dogmatic religion. If *Dharma* be the traditional counterpart of the notion of 'culture', the deepest character of Indian culture could be indicated by quoting '*ayam tu paramo dharmo yad yogenatmadarsanam*', *i.e.* the highest ideal is to seek self-realization through *yoga*. And we could not seek a better or more inclusive definition of *yoga* than what the *Gita* offers, viz., '*yogah karmasu kausalam*', *i.e.*, *yoga* is excellence in work. It may be added that such excellence is traditionally held to require disinterestedness as well as absorption. This subjective modality is as essential to *yoga* or *sadhana* as work itself. In fact, differentiation between them and over-emphasis on one at the expense of the other and then again seeking to reunite them, have led to a dialectical development of alternative modes of spiritual life. This dialectic of *sadhana* is indeed the innermost dialectic of Indian culture. We can thus see the vedic age as one of emphasis on work followed by a long period of the dominance of Gnostic negation *jnana* or *mukti*—and attempts at synthesizing the two ideals of *pravrtti* and *nivrtti*. The pre-eminence of *bhakti* in the middle ages saw the emergence of a new kind of subjectivity in spiritual life just as the 19th and 20th centuries have again sought to rediscover the emphasis on work which the vedas and the *Gita* reveal.

The foregoing reflections may be summed up in a few simple propositions so as to facilitate discussion. Cultural identity can be discovered only from within a cultural consciousness in which the historian needs to participate as a critical observer. The framework for identity will also have to recapitulate the articulation of cultural self-consciousness. Culture again may be defined as an order of values, which aspires after universality but is actually limited by barriers of communication. The communication relevant in this context is not the communication of mere facts or positive knowledge or value-neutral forms. Real cultural communication implies the communication of value as value. This will not necessarily lead to an acceptance of uniform values but will certainly lead to the acceptance of difference and a richer harmony. The spiritual history of India is an illustration of this process. The social ethos which corresponded to this spiritually oriented but multireligious value-pluralism, was naturally one of tolerance and co-existence where different communities with their different traditions were not required to enter any uniform order. This is the social implication of the doctrines of *ahimsa* and *svadharma*. We have again, to note particularly that cultural identity is not a static but a developing thing and that the most important factors influencing it are the inner dialectic of the spiritual quest of the culture and its dialogue with other cultures.

Cultures, however, are necessarily embedded in societies organized for survival and adaptation. This combination of the order of ideal values with the actual order of social organization and all its purposes and pursuits, ideal as well as empirical, has sometimes been called civilization. Civilizations, in this sense, tend to be more universal with respect to their science and technologies than with respect to their values. Upto a point in her history India's civilization constantly absorbed influences creatively from her contacts with other civilizations and remained progressive or alive, but this process apparently slowed down as is apparent from Al-beruni already in the 11th century. This tended to create an imbalance between spiritual creativity and the institutional life of the civilization with the result that by the 19th century Indian culture seemed to find its identity in terms of time-worn stereotypes rather than in terms of the imponderable archetypal creativity underlying them, a confusion which the Renaissance and the Reformation of that century sought to remove through a dialogue with the past as well as with the culture of the West; a task complicated by considerations of politics or fanaticism.

Two

PICTURING INDIA'S PAST : AN AVOIDABLE PITFALL

PRATAP CHANDRA

PIONEERS OF Modern Indian historiography can hardly be blamed if they could not view themselves, and their work detachedly. There are well-recognised limits within which the human mind works. If the pioneers, could have transgressed those limits, they would have seen that they were not responding to a native urge to know the past *qua past*. They were really responding to the alien domination and its apologists. This constituted the basic spring of modern Indian historical endeavour. Western dominance needed to be fought at several levels simultaneously.

A not inconsiderable section of the western historians was, consciously or unconsciously, out to justify and even applaud what the white man was doing to his alleged burden. This required, *inter alia*, a demonstration of the inherent incapacity of the subject people to rule themselves, or to live together peacefully as a well-knit nation-state, with liberalistic values and without an all-consuming mutual hatred. It is an open issue whether history teaches any lesson or not, but it will be difficult to deny that history has always served as a rather effective tool in the making or unmaking of an image. It is equally evident that one type of historical writing can be neutralised only by another. Early Indian historians felt called upon to either go along with the new masters or launch a struggle against them.

Adoption of an inappropriate historical model for the study of Indian history and disregard for the uniqueness of the Indian situation, ironically, resulted from the efforts of both these groups in equal measure. The pro-British historians had no reason to respect India's uniqueness as a nation. Even the so-called nationalist historians failed to do so for two reasons. First, Indian historians, like their western counterparts, viewed history on the analogy of the nineteenth-century physical sciences. They regarded themselves as narrators of wholly and absolutely objective truth that in no way depended on the narrator. They would surely have paid attention to their tacit assumptions and approach had they felt that the historian is not, and indeed cannot be, a passive observer.

Secondly, challenge necessarily conditions the response. If it is weak and does not materially affect the security and/or self-esteen of the challenged, one has the option to meet it or quietly to ignore it. However, when the challenger talks from a position of strength and the threat is real, the challenged can have no alternative but to come forward and meet it squarely or perish. Few, if any, are likely to belong to the latter category. He who opts to deal with the challenger, it may be stressed, is not as free an agent as he might think himself to be. The circumstances oblige him to speak the language of the challenger, use expressions the latter finds easy to comprehend and generally act the role of defendant. He is not free to use his own terminology designed and developed to give expression to his peculiar mode of thinking and dealing with things. These compulsions tend to affect the critical faculties of the challenged to such an extent that he is not able to judge whether it is possible to render what he was to say in an alien terminology. He has got to try. There is no option.

From a joint operation of both these factors resulted a large-scale and uncritical borrowing of concepts, terminology, connotations, values, modes of ratiocination—in short an entire frame of reference—from the alien challenger. A mind not adequately self-critical is bound to succumb to the pressures of powerful aliens. A good deal of early writings on India's political, cultural and ideological histories, therefore, are characterised by odious comparisons, unwarranted conceptual generalisations and a tendency to speak in terms of black and white. Search for a historical model which is based on and respects the uniqueness of Indian situation began only in the recent past when these obstructions began losing their force. On the one hand, the approach to history-writing, experienced a sea-change; on the other, decline of colonialism profoundly affected the psychology of the defendant. Historians all over the world today are a far more introspective, self-conscious and self critical lot than they were ever before. What Collingwood calls 'factology' is definitely on the way out. The unavoidable subjective factors which colour history-writing, and consequently limit historical objectivity are increasingly realised. Not many historians now talk of 'the final history' which Lord Acton seemed to seek and miss. Similarly with the departure of the imperialists and their advocates, Indian historians are no longer reacting. They no longer feel obliged to use history as a mere means to secure an extraneous goal.

A critical insight into the working of the historian's mind has led to a better understanding of the role that analogical reasoning plays as a psychological necessity in the picturing of the unknown or the indirectly known. Developing a historical model means discovering what known situations and factors bear closest resemblance to the situation and factor under study. No one can possibly picture an entirely unknown object, as Locke so convincingly showed. The resemblance, however, may be assumed or posited in two ways : on scanty evidence, or on the basis of a relentlessly critical examination of the entire available material. Unearthing of fresh evidence may lead to modifications in either case. It is apparent that the pioneers, not particularly fastidious about the methods, assumed a great deal without worrying about the evidence. Many of them viewed the Indian situation as if it was a geographical variant of the western, This 'occidentophilia' is now a thing of the past. It was necessary but insufficient for the development of an appropriate model for the study of Indian history. Rejection of the alien does not necessarily lead to an appreciation of the native. A number of pitfalls still need to be guarded against. In this paper I propose to concentrate on only one such pitfall.

History cannot be as objective as the physical sciences (which themselves, after Heisenberg, are no longer supposed to be wholly objective) even in the best of conditions. When it is saddled with a non-historical goal, its limited objectivity suffers a further erosion. One consequence of this erosion is a large-scale confusion of facts and values. 'Facts as reported' form the province of history while values underlie, and influence, all human behaviour. Unlike a layman, the historian is expected to see that his value-judgements and personal preferences do not affect his factual judgements. He is, ideally, a mere reporter. He is supposed to work like a pathologist rather than an advocate. However, comprehension and evaluation are distinguishable only at the hypothetical primitive stage. Once a child acquires some kind of value orientation, he starts judging while he perceives. This is done almost as a reflex action, without deliberation. A herculean effort, consequently is needed to prevent one's value-judgements from interfering with one's capacity to observe. As a person, a historian has every right to cherish his own views regarding good and bad, proper and improper. As a historian, he is required to hold back these views. The demand is obviously far from right, and can be met only by one with a highly trained self-critical mind. However, self-criticism has seldom been the strong-point of a defendant. The moment a charge is levelled, the natural reaction in most cases is to refute it rather than to coolly analyse it and see whether it is based on well-founded assumptions or not. The fact that the denigrator is most likely biased merely sharpens this reaction. This in a way sums up the situation in modern Indian historiography. As counsels for defence, our historians of early days saw nothing wrong in touching up the picture with a view to erase what appeared to them as the weak spots. It did not occur to most of them that what is inapplicable in a given situation can be any thing except its weak spot. I will content myself with two illustrations of how this psychology has worked.

Charge : India was never a single, unified nation-state. She owes her nationhood to the burden-conscious white man.

Implication : If the Indians want to live like one nation, they should co-operate with the alien rulers rather than seek freedom from them. As late as 1920, a celebrated sociologist, Max Weber, by no means an apologist of the empire, predicted that 'a life and death struggle of inimical castes, professions and tribes' would spell the doom of India as a nation as soon as the 'thin conquering strata of the Europeans' was removed.[1] Dark forebodings regarding India's 'imminent break-up' or confident assertions in prestigious foreign journals on election-eves that India was about to have her last election are too familiar to us to need any repetition.

What was our response to this charge? Did we ask, what is so inherently wonderful in being a singularistic nationstate? Is India alone in the category of pluralistic states and societies? Secondly, can there be only one view regarding the nature and character of 'nationhood'? Is it feasible to overlook the historical origins of this concept? We did no such thing. Instead, we set out to assemble 'proofs' to disprove the charge. The over-bearing urge to do so can be gleaned from any textbook of ancient Indian history. Inordinate value was given to politics, central authority and 'imperialism' inspite of the fact that the Indian psyche never considered these to be the be all and end-all of life and in fact did not even mean by these terms what is meant in the West; the non-'imperialist' twelve earliest known 'janapadas' were undervalued at the cost of the four expansionist kingdoms, the Mauryan period of rule was named the 'age of imperial unity'; the western and southern dynasties like the Vakatakas, Cholas and Chalukyas were pushed into the background; Harsha was proclaimed as the 'last great Indian emperor' and so forth.

Similarly, it was not understood that the concept of nation, heavily biased in favour of politics, is the product of a milieu in which politics had prime importance. The Greeks, like ourselves, did not attach much importance to politics. This became fashionable only after the advent of Christianity for reasons we shall soon see. Nation does not necessarily denote either a political entity or a single-tier, uniform object. It primarily connotes a group of those bound together by birth (nate). Such groups are bound to have several dimensions, and there is no reason to think that the social and cultural dimensions are less important than the political. Moreover, large groups tend to promote multi-tier structures, though this does not affect the loyalties to the group as a whole. For instance, an individual owes allegiance at the same time to his part of the state, to the state as a whole, to the linguistic region and finally to the nation, but sees no contradiction in doing so because his loyalty to one does not clash with his loyalty towards another. Total subservience to one entity is, once again, a product of the mentality which underlies Semitic religions.

A unified, singularistic nation-state with a powerful central authority, is, therefore, not a fact in the Indian situation but a value fostered by the aliens. Plurality, multiple-establishments, a determination to stick to form while allowing free development of content, as I have shown elsewhere,[2] are some of the truly Indian characteristics. It is the confusion between facts and values that is responsible for the blurring of the picture. The facts demand that Indian history be treated as the history not of a single, compact nation, but of a sub-continent in which every region has equal importance. Instead of spending our energy on proving that there is something intrinsically great in being ruled from Delhi or some other Indian city, we should try to find out the factors responsible for fostering the uniquely Indian situation.

Charge : India was always religion-dominated *a la* medieval Europe. This explains why she could not develop modern, liberalistic values nor, science.

Consequence : Indian history has been periodized into 'the Hindu period', 'the Mulsim period' and 'the British period' the first two purely in accordance with the religion of the alleged central authority.

Assumption : Religion and politics are two sides of the same coin. If the ruler was Hindu, could the ruled be anything else?

The terms 'Hindu' and 'Muslim' have lately been replaced by 'ancient' and 'medieval', but I feel that the fixation with religion is very much there in the minds of both professional and amateur historians. The lack of a holistic approach is partly responsible for this. Communication among historians specialising in different branches has, regrettably, been scanty. If those dealing with Indian thought display little understanding of socio-political milieu, the political historians pay little attention to the nature and character of religion. Use of the term 'religion' in the singular indicates that all religions are thought to be alike. They are not alike. Students of comparative religions make a clear distinction between two types. One group, to which Christianity and Islam belong, works on the assumption that everything has been created by one personal God for a purpose. This makes it obligatory for all created beings to work for the furtherance of that purpose. This group must logically accord high priority to the efforts to shape society in one particular way. Politics is a natural corollary of these religions. Religions of India belong to an altogether different genre. Several eminent authorities have noticed this. R.C. Zaehner writes, "Religions of Semitic origins are forever proclaiming the Truth—one and undivided. For the Hindu truth is a many sided affair and can be viewed from many angles. Semitic religions are ideologies : Hinduism and Buddhism are ways of life"[3]. Added to this is the fact that for Hindus and Buddhists, the world is neither the creation of an all powerful and benevolent God, nor has it any purpose. All talk of deliverance from the rounds of existence would become incomprehensible if this is lost sight of.

The kind of importance given to religion in India's political history largely stems from ignoring this basic difference. The fundamental assumptions of Indian religions make politics superfluous for them. Religion has always been strictly apolitical in India, something intensely personal—no matter whether the believer is a ruler or a subject. Unlike the West, the ruler's religion did not automatically become the religion of the ruled. A political era can justifiably be given a religious tag only when religion plays some role in politics.

How did something so obvious come to be overlooked? The answer is simple. Lack of religious fanaticism means free thinking and liberalism—a product of the Renaissance. For various, predominantly ahistorical, reasons, early Western and Indian historians decided to view India in the mirror of medieval Europe. Once this analogy became fixed in their minds, the rest followed as a matter of course. Indians became intolerant fanatics. A single and all-powerful established viewpoint came to be posited. Terms like orthodox and heterodox, mainstream and minor currents started exerting deep influence on the historian's imagination. This picture was both simple and familiar to most western historians; no wonder they found it so suitable. Our own inability to subject it to a critical appraisal helped perpetuate it down the ages to the extent that it has now become more or less axiomatic.

It is time that greater attention was paid to facts as known through extant sources instead of making do with such borrowed models. It should be realised that the communal problem in its present form is not due to, but in contravention of the truly Indian spirit, a result of India's response to the Semitic challenge. If Max Weber and other 'well-wishers' of India have been consistently proved wrong, the reason lies in their total inability to understand this basic feature of the Indian psyche. A somewhat rigid social structure was India's answer to the peculiar geographic-ethnic situation obtaining in the early days. But this cannot obliterate the fact that attempts to force a particular ideology on any one are conspicuous only by their total absence in India. What a person believes is entirely his or her business so long as the belief does not tend to weaken the social fabric. There is no justification for allowing our reaction to the former to colour our understanding of the latter. After all, form and content are not the same thing.

References

1 Weber, Max, *The Religion of India : The Sociology of Hinduism and Buddhism,* translated and edited by H.H. Gerth and D. Martindale, Glemcoe : The Free Press, 1958, p. 325.

2. See the author's *The Hindu Mind,* Simla : I.I.A.S. 1977 ; 'Ideological Discord in Ancient India', *Dissent and Protest in Indian Civilization,* edited by S.C. Malik, I.I.A.S., Simla, 1977, 'Ideological Discord : Protest or Plurality?' *Quest* 99, Jan-Feb., 1976.

3. cf. Zaehner, R.C., *At Sundry Times,* Faber and Faber, London, 1958, p. 20; Weber, Max, op. cit. p. 21 ; Warder, A.K., *An Introduction to Indian Historiography,* Bombay, Popular, 1972, p. 9.

CONFLICT AND CONSENSUS

Three

CONSENSUS AND CONFLICT : SOME CONSIDERATIONS*

K.J. SHAH

I. Introduction

FOR THIS paper, I am going to assume that history is not merely a chronicle of events (and it is doubtful if even a chronicle of events can be merely a chronicle of events), and that it involves an understanding of what has happened. Any such understanding of events presupposes an understanding of the nature of man and society—either implicitly or explicitly. Differences in the understanding of the nature of man and society produce different accounts of the events of the same time and place. (I am not referring to the differences in personal background and temperament which might produce such differences given the same understanding of the nature of man and society; nor am I concerned with the fact that the differences in background and temperament affect the choice of a particular understanding of the nature of man and society). I want to concern myself with a particular kind of difference in the understanding of history. In the light of this, I consider the role of consensus and conflict in society.

*This paper, read and discussed in the March, '78 seminar of the Indian History and Culture Society was published in *Indian Philosophical* Quarterly, Poona, Vol. VI, no. 1, Oct., '78 for which an acknowledgement to the I.H.C.S. will be made in the succeed ing number of the I.P.Q.

This could have been done by undertaking a detailed examination of a case which illustrates the kind of difference in understanding that I am going to consider. For various reasons, I have not been able to do this. I have tried to overcome this shortcoming by beginning with a reference to a case-study which might clarify some of the points I make in the paper in an abstract manner. The case study considers the differences in understanding and reactions of Gandhiji and Ambedkar to the problem of untouchability. Some of the main points are presented in the next section.

After this I briefly present two models of man and society and their bearing on our understanding of history. One model views man and society in terms of the mutual interaction and determination of several factors—the dominance of any factor is not a matter of principle, but only a temporary empirical phenomenon. The other model views man and society in terms of the dominance of one factor or another which mainly determines other factors and makes man and society what they are. In the next section I consider some problems of the use of these models. On the basis of these considerations, I suggest that the more fundamental conflict is between the comprehensive and partial models rather than between consensus and conflict as methods of dealing with problems and point out the relation of the two models to the theme of consensus and conflict.

II. The Case-Study : Untouchability and the Different Presuppositions of Gandhi and Ambedkar

In a paper I wrote some time ago (Dissent, protest and Reform : some Conceptual Considerations—in Dissent, Protest and Reform in Indian Civilization, 1977, Indian Institute of Advanced Study, Simla) I have studied the presuppositions of Gandhi and Ambedkar in their understanding and tackling of the problem of untouchability. I have argued there that Gandhiji was not concerned with only the economic, political and social positions of the untouchables; he was also concerned with their moral and spiritual life. Further, Gandhi was not concerned only with all the aspects of the life of the Harijans, he was also concerned with all the aspects of life of the Caste Hindus and the non-Hindus. As against this Ambedkar was concerned with the economic, political and social life of the Harijans and not with the moral and religious aspects of their lives; and he was concerned with the life of the Harijans and not with that of the Caste Hindus. In the reactions, Ambedkar was vehement, but Gandhi was firm; so far as fight is concerned Gandhi was also ready to fight. However, Ambedkar was impatient to see the lot of the Harijan improved, whereas Gandhi was keen on dealing with problems so that further problems, equally or more difficult, were not created.

It would be wortnwhile to go into the details of how this affected their understanding, the consequences of their actions and their vision of the future.

III. Two Models of Understanding of Man and Society :

In this section I briefly sketch two models of understanding of man and society. They are importantly different but related. I present these models in the framework of *purusharthas*—the goals of man, *dharma*, *artha*, *kama and moksha*. I do this for many reasons. Among them are; this understanding of man represents the traditional understanding of man which is not absent from our present day life. However, what is more important, it is a comprehensive understanding of man capable of systematic use in the understanding of man and society.

The understanding of man in terms of purusharthas raises many questions such as : What is the nature of these goals? Are these the only possible goals? etc. However, for our purposes, it is not necessary to go into these questions. But we must note a few points :

a) The purusharthas are a group of interacting factors in a matrix; and the goal is to attain not only moksha but all the goals together in an integrated manner.

b) It is important to note some relationships between the attainment of different goals. For this purpose, let us order the goals in an increasing order of importance artha, kama, dharma and moksha. It is possible, though not necessary, that an individual may pursue any goal of lesser importance– say artha and neglect a goal of higher importance. But a person who pursues a goal of higher importance, say moksha, must include the attainment of all the other lower goals –say artha, kama and dharma. The pattern of integration of the goals varies from person to person combining the goals in many ways.

c) Given these goals of the individual we can consider the goals of the society. (This is an unsatisfactory way of putting things, because the goals of the individual presuppose the goals of the society and *vice-versa.*) A broad description of the goals of the society would be that it seeks to facilitate the realisation of the individual's goals. It need not be emphasised that facilitation does not mean attainment of the goals.

d) The facilitation of the attainment of the goals does not mean the same thing in respect of the different goals. In respect of artha, kama and dharma (in the attainment of artha and kama and one aspect of dharma) the role of the society is direct; that is, the role of the society is direct in the integration of the pursuit of these goals by the members of the community. In respect of dharma (in so far as it is related to the attainment of moksha) and moksha, the role of the society is indirect, *i.e.* the role of the society is indirect in the integration of the pursuit of the goals in the individual himself. However, it is necessary that the society should so organise itself that the pursuit of a goal—say, artha—does not by its manner or by its hardships or its ease make it too difficult to attain the moral or the religious goal. Equally, of course, the pursuit of the moral or religious life should not make the attainment of the material goals of the community too difficult.

However, it is a point of considerable importance that this facilitation can be made not for the individuals as such —their differences are too many and too detailed—but for individuals as members of groups. Here too, society does not consider all possible groups and their claims for example, until very recently, the homesexuals were not recognized as a group. However, the recognized groups would cover all the individuals, though not perhaps in all their aspects. In this framework, the individual was supposed to take care of his own problems. (Incidentally, this has a bearing on the understanding of sarvodaya). It is understood as well-being of all the groups rather than that of all the individuals, it gives a different orientation to questions of social policy.

The Second Model : As we had said earlier, the second model also uses the framework of purusharthas. It also accepts that there is inter-relationship between these goals. However, it gives a predominant role to a particular factor so that it largely, if not wholly, determines the pursuit of the various goals by the members of the community.

This basic importance given to a particular factor must be distinguished from the importance given to a particular factor for different reasons. For example, at a particular time, in particular circumstances, a particular factor—economic, technological—may be very important on account of significant changes. In these circumstances, to give special attention to a particular factor will not be incompatible with the first model or again, a historian may be interested in a particular aspect of the life of the community. This also will not be incompatible with the acceptance of the first model. What is incompatible with the first model is the determining role assigned to one factor generally and universally.

Given this kind of understanding of man and society, our view of the history of the society would be different from the one given to us by the first model. It will direct the attention of the individual or the society or both to the attainment of a particular goal. If the importance is given to the moral or religious goal, the facilitating role of the institutions will be forgotten; and if the importance is given to the material goals; the institutions will be given a determining role rather than a facilitating role; and the role of the individual will be forgotten.

IV. The Two Models and Their Application

In this section, I consider some problems in the use of these models and some tentative applications of the models.

1. In the account of the models, there is an important confusion which needs to be cleared up. It is not at all clear whether the goals or the predominance of a particular goal represents a particular situation or it represents an ideal. What do the models say—that such and such is the state of affairs or that such and such ought to be the state of affairs?

The manner of putting the question suggests that the account has to be understood either in terms of the actual or in terms of the ideal. However, I think that this is to misunderstand the nature of the models. Each model's claim is to represent man and society as they are—in a state of health. If they are not in a state of health, then they are sick—in a state of aberration; and they ought to be restored to health. In this context, it is wrong to make a sharp contrast between "is" and "ought".

2. But now the question will be; who decides what is health? Who decides which of the two models represents health? Is this a matter of personal choice? Or are there criteria by means of which we could decide in favour of one or the other?

One of the criteria suggested might be that the true account of health may be distinguished from the false account by considering which of the two leads us to understand and deal with the situations. However, such an answer reveals only a further question—what is it to deal with a situation? In a certain sense of the term, both the models will enable one to deal with the situation. (Let us remember that both Gandhi and Ambedkar dealt with the situation.) And both the ways may have their limitations and their merits.

The disadvantage of the comprehensive model is that it makes action difficult; but it has the advantage of being thorough. The advantage of the partial model is that action is easier, however it is not thorough. It deals with only a particular aspect of the problem and, therefore, it is likely that further problems might arise. It seems therefore that what is good in theory is not so good in practice, or what is good in practice is not so good in theory. But this only means that we must be wrong in our view either of what is good theory or of what is good practice. I am going to assume that the comprehensive model gives us both good theory and good practice. The limitations of practice are only temporary. The partial model is bad both in theory and practice. The advantages of practice are only apparent and temporary. (Though I have said that I am assuming this, the considerations in the next section will show that considerations can be advanced in favour of this assumption).

V. The Two Models and Consensus and Conflict :

How are these two models of the understanding of society related to the theme of consensus and conflict? In order to answer this question, I should like to distinguish between two ways in which the concepts of consensus and conflict may be understood. In one of the ways, they refer to the mode of setting a conflict. In consensus, an agreement is arrived at though the nature of the agreement could vary greatly. In conflict, a solution to a dispute is sought by fighting it out—legally, in parliament etc. But consensus and conflict represent two different modes of understanding society. In the consensus mode of understanding, a dispute or a problem is understood in terms of all the interests and of all the groups. In the conflict mode of understanding, a dispute or a problem is understood in terms of a particular interest and of a particular group. The former mode emphasizes cooperation, the latter mode conflict. One might say that the consensus mode of understanding may lead to the consensus method, and the conflict mode of understanding to the conflict method; but there is no necessary relationship between the modes of understanding and the methods bearing the corresponding names. The method of setting a problem will depend on the tradition and circumstances of the society, whatever the mode of the understanding of the problem.

If I am right, our emphasis should not be so much on the method, but on the mode of understanding. We must go in for consensus as a mode of understanding rather than conflict. We must prefer consensus rather than conflict also as a method. But if necessary, conflict in the service of consensus understanding, is to be preferred to consensus in favour of the conflict mode of understanding.

VI. Some Concluding Remarks

1. If the distinction between the two models in terms of health and disease is accepted, the criteria in terms of which we judge of the progress of a society will be altered. We would not judge of the progress of a society in terms only of a particular aspect of life.

2. In the light of the considerations presented here, I believe, it is plausible to suggest that a particular misunderstanding was an important factor in the decline of the Hindus : the misunderstanding being that if an individual can be indifferent to artha and kama in the pursuit of moksha, a society also can be.

3. It will also alter the understanding of our present problems and their solutions.*

*I am grateful to Dr. K. Raghavendra Rao for his comments and suggestions which have helped me in reducing the unclarities and mistakes of Commission and omission in the paper.

Four

A PERSPECTIVE OF INTEGRATION

R.N. MISRA

INDIA TODAY is caught in a web of tensions which are creations of her own history[1]. While the problems may not be new, the circumstances are. Although every historical situation is unique, but a broader appraisal of its cyclical or linear tradition may be helpful in understanding the problems and solving them. Keeping this in view, a brief survey of our ancient social and political system is attempted here, within the framework of the geographical entity of our country.

'*Bharatavarsha*' in its broader geophysical dimensions came to be visualised in the Epics and the Puranas[2], although even prior to these texts a political unification of the country was achieved during the rule of the Nandas and the Mauryas. The *Manusmriti* conceives of Bharatavarsha as consisting of two cultural divisions—*aryavarta* and *daksinapatha*. Patriotic sentiments extolling the country of invoking its unity are never wanting[3]. The Puranas sometimes describe the segments of the country and then encompass them together, thus affirming its unity. For instance, the *Nilamata Purana* (V. 7.11), mentions nine divisions of the country and affirms their individual and collective sanctity[4]. The diversity of the country is referred to in the *Kurma Purana* (47.19) which at the same time, recognises its unity also. In fact, such recognition of unity is present all the time and the heterogenous elements are bound together with the help of consciously created elements for fostering unity. One such element was : ruler, or in a wider sense, the State. Ancient Indian political philosophy enjoins the establishment of hegemony as a moral obligation for rulers, and those who abided by it were promised spiritual glory A monarch is advised to visualise his state *vis-a-vis* the other states peripheral to his own as constituting a hypothetical *mandala*[5]. It is said that considering himself as the centre of the *mandala*, a prince should exercise his military and political force to his best advantage and maintain a balance of power beneficial to himself[6]. A centralised and strong state but mindful of the susceptibilities of feudatories and their local conditions was regarded as ideal in ancient India and most of the ancient treatises on political theory—from the *Arthasastra* of Kautilya to the *Nitivakyamrita* of Somadeva support it.

Though the king has been described as the initiator of the *yuga-raja kalasya karanam*-ancient Indian society kept the initiative to itself in vital matters. The sastras recognize princes only in their position as executors of law of the land. The authority of framing laws was vested in the sages. The system, thus, had an in-built safeguard against the waywardness of princes. As regards the sages, while they upheld the traditional political and social system, they also devised ways and means to accommodate new situations that arose with the passage of time. They counselled kings as well as commoners. Their significance as an integrating force cannot be doubted. We give a few examples.

The *varnasrama dharma* had always been dear to ancient law-givers. The rulers were enjoined to enforce it with full vigour and they took pride in doing so for they often claimed that when the *varnasrama dharma* wilted under pressure they resurrected it by their own efforts[7]. The system did uphold the ancient social fabric. When new situations challenged the system, ways and means were readily devised by the sages to accommodate them. There are references to indicate that foreigners were sometimes regarded as a polluting factor if they held land under their sway. Such regions came to be regarded as unfit for the performance of Vedic sacrifices and rituals[8]. Eventually the law-givers not only accommodated outsiders in the social fold but also gave them respectable status. Legends were developed to legitimise their presence. They were regarded as descendants of Anu and Turvasu, the two sons of Yayati. The *Tandya Brahmana* prescribed the vratyastoma ceremony to incorporate them[9]. Manu regarded them as 'fallen Ksatriyas' and explained that the reason for it was their disregard of the sastras. Assimilation of the pre-Turkish foreigners was total. The Magian sun-worshippers of Iran were accepted as *sakadvipi Brahamanas*[10]. The *agnikula* legend gave sanction to several ruling dynasties of foreign extraction. Ancient inscriptions refer to matrimonial relations of Indian rulers with them[11]. The Dahiya Rajputs and the Tegins or Shahi Tegins also became part of the ancient social system. The former had come from the vicinity of the Caspian Sea; the latter seem to have been ancient Iranians[12]. A natural acceptance of these communities could not have been possible without the support of the ancient Indian orthodox system. As an Institution sages and seers were highly venerated in the ancient political set up. From the Vedic times onwards sages were always included among the kings' counsellors. In the middle ages a peculiar practice is observed according to which rulers donated their states to their royal preceptors and ruled in proxy for their spiritual *gurus*[13].

In the domain of religious history also a dynamic process of growth is noticed. Among the major religious systems of India there were sects and sub-sects representing many shades of opinion. It has been aptly said that "... every passage in Hindu sacred texts is open to figurative interpretation so that it is possible for different schools of Hinduism to hold diametrically opposed doctrines without any serious antagonism"[14]. A closer examination of sects indicates instances of rivalry and antagonism; these stresses however could never jeopardise the ancient religious system. Through the Agamic to the Vedic we find several basic changes in approaches to the fundamental tenets of religion. It has been remarked that "in the Vedic (religion) the doer (*karta*) occupies the central position in the scheme of life whereas God or his grace have no place...(while in the Agamic theological view) God, Grace and Heaven are in the centre ..and man has been placed in the peripheric region"[15]. Such a conviction was responsible for the development of theistic cults in medieval times, and in its popular appeal carried almost the whole country with it.

Sometimes the sages launched crusades against the ills in society through their discourses and gathered immense support. The Buddha for example made a strong case against the relevance of a social order based on the *varna* system, thus : "there is no inherent virtue in belonging to a particular *varna*; a Brahmana was not born from sky or air, nor did he spring direct from earth; just as a Chandala is born of his mother's womb so is a Brahmana. All men are just the same and in their limbs there is no distinctive feature to necessitate the four fold division of the *varnas*. Nor is there any need to accept this division just because a Brahmana prescribes it". The Buddha proclaimed equality of all men. The Bhakti movement preached the same philosophy of equality of all men and in regard to devotion and rituals it prescribed personal identification with the Deity rather than observance of intricate rituals[16]. As a source of socio-religious synthesis the Bhakti movement was a force to be reckoned with. Even as these developments were taking place the orthodox section attempted to bring about a synthesis by invoking monotheistic sentiments. The *Skanda Purana*[17] for instance calls the creator as one, saying : *sa cha Narayanah smritah sa Sivo nasti bhedastesham parasparam;*

The institution of *tirtha-yatra* was also a factor of synthesis in the ancient religious scheme and it helped in bringing people of farflung regions together. The practice of *panchopasana* served the same purpose. The fact that medieval sculptures offer us a large number of syncretic icons[18] incorporating the features and attributes of different deities also indicates that attempts were made towards achieving religious harmony.

Ancient texts take note of the differences in the cultural patterns of different regions, but prescribe their preservation. For instance the *Jivanamukti Viveka informs* us that the *brahmanas* of the north were censured by the *brahmanas* of the south for relishing non-vegetarian food; the latter in their turn were reproached for cross-cousin marriages or for taking earthen vessels on pilgrimage. As regards the function of the ruler in such situations he is advised to preserve local customs in conformity with the traditions of *desa*, *kula* and *jati*. It is also stated that if local customs were in contravention of dharma they continued to remain sinful despite the non-intervention of state for the purpose of punishment.

A study of the ancient Indian socio-political system indicates that total harmony never existed, neither perhaps it was the goal. Society kept adjusting itself to situations that arose from time to time, by offering solutions to preserve the social structure. It may be said that problems were usually institution-bound; when they grew weak, they became sources of disharmony. Their longevity is proof of their tenacity caused by various factors.

References

1. Bharatavarsha was a developing entity. Sometimes a part of the country was praised while another was disparaged. This may have been caused by the disparate ethnic composition of the people of respective regions. The parochialism, however, disappeared with the passage of time.
2. *Brihad Naradiya Purana,* III, 47.
3. *Vishnu Purana,* II. 3. 24 ; *Varaha Purana*, 88, 68.
4. *Kurma Purana* XXXV. 708.
5. cf. Misra, R.N., "The Dynamic Mandala", *Journal of M.P. Historical* Society, V. pp. 39, 43.
6. ibid.
7. *Vishnu Smriti,* 84, p. 525 ; Kane, P.V., *The History of Dharma-shastra,* II, 937 ; IV, 378 ff.
8. ibid, II (ii), pp. 386 ff.
9. cf, Vishvakosa., (Hindi) sv. Maga ; *Brithatsamhita,* LX. 19 ; Pathak, V.S., *Madhya Bharati,* VIII, (8) part 1, p. 4.
10. Pathak, V.S. Ibid.
11. Ibid.,
12. Pathak, V.S. "Kalachuri Rajaguruon ki parampara", (Hindi) *Madhya Bharati* (Univ. of Saugar 1958) p.1.
13. Basham, A.L., *Studies in Indian History and Culture* (Calcutta, 1964) P. 13.

14. Pathak, V.S., *Madhya Bharati*, VIII part 1, section A. 1959, p. 6.
15. Divyavadana, p. 328.
16. *Skanda Purana*, VII, ii. 18.41.
17. cf., Banerjea, J.N., *The Development of Hind Iconography*, Calcutta, 1956, see Syncretic Icons.
18. f., Kane, P.V., op. cit. Vol. III, pp. 857-862, also 849 ff.

Five

CONFLICT AND CONSENSUS IN INDIAN CIVILIZATION

DEVAHUTI

THE ORIGIN of the conflict model is to be traced to the Marxian dialectical theory and action. Both in respect of the dialectical method, and the material basis of history Marx had predecessors, but it was his system which most sharply brought the theories in focus and directly influenced the writing of history. The force behind the dialectic of history was the class struggle. A questioning of the conflict model logically leads, first to the assumption, and then a critical examination of the consensus model. We shall attempt to do so in the context of Indian civilization.

Marx's general principle of an organic process of transformation and development is demonstrated through the process conflict-consensus. Within consensus new conflicts arise to give birth to a new consensus and so on. One is implicit in the other. Emphasis on one or the other, however, can lead to important differences in the interpretation of the same phenomena. Assumptions, methods, and aim lead to the choice of emphasis in the study of history.[1] On our part we shall try to see if, in our context, conflict took place within the general framework of consensus or consensus occurred in the general framework of conflict.

In the ancient, and largely also in the medieval milieu in India, (milieu being fashioned by the physical environment, kinship patterns, technology, aesthetics, religion, and the predominantly agrarian economy of the times) the emphasis appears to have been on consensus *i.e.* adjustment, give and take, synthesis or at least an *active acceptance* of co-existence. This is manifest through various mediums. Our conclusion is reached by testing our hypothesis on the developmental pattern of some aspects of Indian history, eg. ethnic, linguistic, artistic and religious.

There was considerable ethnic commingling prompted probably both by will and necessity, inspite of the size of the country and difficulties of communication, but aided by the time factor. For the third and second millennium B.C., there is anthropometric evidence, supported by stone and bronze figures that the Proto-Australoid, the Paleo-Mediterranean and probably also the Caspian (Proto-Nordic) comprised the Harappan population.[2] With the emergence of the Vedic Aryans another element was added. The Mahabharata, being an epic, and incorporating a lot of folk and bardic lore of both earlier and contemporary times refers to many types of intermarriages as well as to plural settlements and habitations. The Gita's pre-occupation with the containment of the *varna samkara* phenomenon may in part be a response to the crisis of the times when social mobility in terms of region, race and *varna* had reached a saturation point endangering the preservation of cultural identity of the groups as they then stood. Today it is mainly the cultural exterior comprising clothes and adornments that gives away the regionality of a man or woman rather than distinctive physical traits. Probably that has been so for the last two thousand years as the greatest intermixing of peoples took place in the very early stages of man's history.

Another medium through which consensus expressed itself was script and language. Both Tamil and Sanskrit, and naturally all the related languages of later times adopted the Brahmi script.

Regarding interchange between languages and through them of ideas, the Negrito elements are present only in the Andamans (and beyond in South-east Asia), but words from the speech of the proto-Australoids exercised considerable influence both on the Dravidian and Sanskrit groups. Examples range from the Kol or Munda *jom*, 'to eat' (Hindi, jeem), Kol *marak*, peacock (compare Dravidian *mayil*), *bana* (arrow), *laguda*, *linga* (digging stick, phallus), to counting on the basis of 20 (*kodi*), reckoning of days by the phases of the moon (raka—full moon, kuhu—new moon), and probably the name of one constellation—*matrika* (the Pleiades, Polynesian *matariki*).[3] As for the Tamil loan words in Sanskrit - British, American and Dutch scholars have demonstrated their use even in the earliest Veda.[4] That Tamil borrowed from Sanskrit in the matter of vocabulary as well as construction and had done so at a very early stage has also been shown.[5]

The advent of regional languages in the medieval period, partly a conflict phenomenon, has to be viewed in the light of several factors, not the least of which is the fact that *prakrits* had existed and flourished from the earliest times.

Art, whether of the ancient or the medieval period also demonstrates consensus. The various schools of architecture, sculpture, and painting are only convenient divisions, thus the south-north classification. They do not run along parallel lines, they criss-cross at various planes and have vastly more in common than in contradiction, especially in the ancient period.

This is not surprising in view of the wide circulation of texts as well as of artists and craftsmen. *Silpa* and *vastu* sastras[6] composed in different regions were used over the entire length and breadth of the country including the difficult Himalayan terrain, and beyond the seas in South-east Asia.

The *Katha-kosha* records[7] the name of an architect Sura-deva who designed a temple in Pataliputra and kept its model in Sopara, a west coast port, north of Bombay, where he was resident, on view for future clients.

Guilds of artisans and families of painters migrated from region to region, (and once again beyond India, to South-east Asia also[8]) according to demand and owing to other factors. They naturally carried their traditions with them although they fully responded to the local environments and heritage, in terms of materials, designs, and motifs.[9]

The Bodh Gaya temple survives as a solitary example of the so-called southern school in northern India.

For the medieval period, while dozens of monuments exhibit a harmonious blend of Hindu and Islamic features in a gradual pattern of development over the centuries, both at the centre and in the states, the most striking example is provided by the Govind Deo temple[10] at Brindaban built in 1590. It has incorporated domes and arches in the interior and has almost completely eschewed sculptural figures in the exterior.

Religion, perhaps, offers the largest area of consensus. The synthesis of the *agama*, and *nigama*, the *dasavatara* theory, the adoption of *yoga* in idea and practice by widely different schools from *Sankhya*, to *Bhakti*, to *Tantra*, the growth under a common arche-type of a diversity of sects such as the *Kapalika*, *Siddhantin*, *Nayanar* and *Lingayata*—all *Saiva*, the acceptance in general of the myths, deities and symbols of one tradition by the other and the adoption of common behavioral patterns and institutions are some of the many examples of consensus in religion. Even the Buddha, the most distinguished of dissenters continued to use the old term *brahmana* to denote the ideal man[11] along with its use as a counter-category to *sramana*.

To some consensus means conservatism, lack of the spirit of adventure, and compromise on principles. To others it is evidence of a practical sense in making use of the existing reality. It takes the harder road of resilience and also indicates strength and self confidence in being able to cope with the weight of tradition.

We started with the assumption that conflict is implicit in consensus. To demonstrate consensus, therefore, is not to, (1) rule out instances of conflict for short periods in some areas at any time in Indian history although they would be much easier to spot in the relatively recent past, not having had time to be affected by the predominant trait of consensus, nor to, (2) stop wishing for conflict in the future. But it is (1) to stop applying wishful tninking to the past, (2) to stop using alien-in-time and-in-space categories, valid for their own times and places, to Indian civilization in general.

It seems to me that the leap pattern in history has been absent in India because of inbuilt dissent. Variety is dissent. The consensus, has been on accepting dissent, conflict.

References

1. One set of assumptions, methods, and aim may respectively be : antagonism of classes, a linear and graduated view of the process of struggle, and the logical result of the process—victory of one over the other. The other set may consist of a neutral, non-positive view of the process thus : non-antagonistic, non-linear, non-graduated (*i.e.* continuous), non-victory, etc.
2. *Memoirs Anthropological Sur. India*, vol.. 9, 1962.
3. S.K. Chatterji, "Recent Movements and Prehistoric Culture" in *The Vedic Age* (ed.) R.C. Majumdar, p. 152.
4. T. Burrow and M.B. Emeneau, *A Dravidian Etymological Dictionary*, Oxford, 1961 ; T. Burrow, "Loan words in Sanskrit", Trans. Philogical Soc., 1946, pp. 1-30 ; M.B. Emeneau, "Linguistic Pre-history in India" P.A.P.S. 98, 1954, pp. 282-92. J. Gonda, *Four Studies in the Language of the Veda*, 1959.
5. T. Burrow, "Dravidian Studies", B.S.O.A.S. 1938-48 ; M.B. Emeneau and T. Burrow, *Dravidian Borrowings from Indo-Aryan*, Berkeley, 1962.
6. The names of some that have survived are the Visva-karmayam, Mayamatam, Kasyapam, Brahmiyam, Sarasvatiyam, Mana-saram, etc.
7. Tr. C.H. Tawney, p. 150.
8. There is inscriptional evidence supported by a Jaina literary source for master sculptors of different generations but of common lineage working in India and South-east Asia. *Cor. Ins. Ind.* IV, pt. 1, no. 62 and pt. 2, no. 105.
9. In addition to other sources we acknowledge our debt to R.N. Mishra's paper on Temples in Madhya Pradesh read at a seminar at the IIAS, Simla in 1975 and B.N. Goswami's paper on Pahari Paintings read at a seminar at the Himachal Pradesh State Museum, Simla, 1976.
10. Percy Brown, *Indian Architecture I*, p. 129, plate cxv, fig. 2.
11. Brahmana-vagga in the *Dhamma-pada.*

It seems [illegible] that the [illegible] pattern in history has been absent in India [illegible] dissent. Variety is [illegible] dissent. The consensus has been on accepting dissent [illegible]

Reference[illegible]

1. [illegible]
2. [illegible]
3. [illegible]
4. [illegible] Oxford [illegible]
5. [illegible]
6. [illegible]
7. [illegible] p. 250.
8. [illegible]
9. [illegible] Mishra's [illegible]
10. [illegible]
11. [illegible]

Six

CONFLICT AND CONSENSUS IN THE STUDY OF INDIAN NATIONALISM

SUDHIR CHANDRA

A SUBJECTIVE phenomenon that emerged in response to a variety of objective factors, nationalism represented a new unifying principle that cut across traditional units of social cohesion within Indian society even as it was influenced by them. This new principle owed its existence to a two-fold process : first, progressive awareness of an underlying conflict between what came to be seen as Indian and British or national and imperial interests; and, second, rationalisation of narrow group interests as national interests. Paradoxically, therefore, from its very nascence nationalism carried within it possibilities of both cohesion and disruption. Gradually, the material aspect tended to be eclipsed — in terms of visibility — by the unfoldment of nationalism as an ideology representing the elemental human urge for freedom.

A significant feature of the historiography of Indian nationalism has been that in its two main manifestations it proceeds from preconceptions about the national capacity or incapacity of Indian society to be charged with the unifying principle of nationalism. One trend within this historiography proceeds on the assumption of Indian national unity; the other on its negation. Another significant point to be noted is that in addition to this preconception, much of the controversy surrounding this historiography has sprung from the tendency of most scholars to concentrate either on the ideological or on the material aspect of the emergence and development of nationalism.

As early as 1885 the nature of confrontation between nationalism and imperialism was grasped in two diametrically different ways by Henry Cotton and John Seeley. While Cotton's *New India* enunciated the dynamics of a self-liquidating imperialism fostering and preparing the ground for nationalism, Seeley's *The Expansion of England* posited a hostile, dichotomous relationship between imperialism and nationalism. Here, in fact, were the prototypes of what emerged as the Tory and Liberal schools of imperialist historiography of India.

What Indians did was to react sharply to Seeley and to derive sustenance from Cotton. Since then Indian writings on Indian nationalism have generally been marked by an almost obsessive concern for national unity. It is a measure of the strength of this obsession that even the Marxian historiography in India has not been free from this nationalist bias.[1] Anything that seemed to threaten unity was, as it continues to be, attacked instead of being rationally comprehended.[2]

An essential result of such an attitude was that attention was focused on the ideological aspect of nationalism. Not only was the material aspect blurred, indeed overlooked; nationalism was invested with a sacred idealism. Naturally, nationalism was explained in terms of an ever widening consensus within Indian society. Areas of conflict were left unlocated.

But, given the course of the Indian national movement, this could not be done beyond a point. The emergence of the All India Muslim League and the eventual creation of Pakistan made some recognition, and explanation, of conflict inevitable. The ways in which this was largely sought to be done further stresses the tenacity with which the ideological aspect of nationalism was clung to. One of these ways was to attribute Muslim communalism—it is significant that the term given to the phenomenon was communalism and not separatism or nationalism—to the sinister imperialist policy of divide and rule. The other was to introduce religion as the principle that distinguished and kept apart Hindus and Muslims as two mutually antagonistic cultural communities which had obstinately refused to work out a process of synthesis. The most respectable development of this trend can be seen in the X and XI volumes of the *History and Culture of the Indian People* brought out by the Bharatiya Vidya Bhavan. Of course, religion cannot be written off as of no efficacy as a motivating factor. But to attempt to explain such complex phenomena as national integration and disintegration exclusively or even largely in terms of religion is to overlook the material genesis of the ideological manifestations of a conflict.

The pervasiveness of this religious orientation can be gauged from the fact that it colours the writings of even an eminent nationalist historian like the late Sardar K.M. Panikkar. For he wrote, to give but one example : '...the Hindu people it can never too strongly be emphasised, constitute the basis of Indian history and culture'.

If the general trend in India has been towards highlighting pseudo-conflict and let the *facade* of consensus hide the areas of real conflict, the most important western trend, as represented by the Cambridge school of Indian history, has magnified conflict within Indian society and underplayed inordinately the consensus that was emerging in the form of nationalism. While earlier this school attempted to highlight caste as a factor of conflict, the focus now is on the pursuit of power by interest groups operating within the patron-client model at the local, provincial and national levels, and united by vertical linkages. Because ideology is recognised as too obtrusive, an element to be conveniently set aside, verbal recognition is extended to its importance without the basic argument being affected by it. Naturally, the Cambridge school, too, offers only a tilted image of the reality of nationalism. It fails to account for a consensus that was much wider than the consensus represented by interest groups, their various linkages notwithstanding.

In recent years, however, some worth while studies have appeared—but only some—in which the inextricable inter-connections of power, interest and ideology have been taken into consideration with a view to understanding Indian nationalism in its totality, and to view Indian nationalism in terms of both consensus and conflict.[3] But these attempts fall outside the main stream of Indian history writing. The general approach to the study of Indian nationalism in our country continues to be inspired by the belief that nationalism was something sacred.

Necessary though it seemed to briefly indicate the main lines on which the historiography of Indian nationalism has developed, my own interest in consensus and conflict as factors of analysis of nationalism is in relation to their effect. Generally, conflict and consensus have been so employed as to generate patriotic pride or to sustain imperialistic hangover. In this sense, most of this historiography has been conservative in its effect; and it has been so in spite of its basically conflicting drives.

The imperialistic bias may be left alone, even though it informs the work of some well-known Indian historians as well. But the stress, in Indian writings, on nationalism as an ideology, an ideology that often borders dangerously on chauvinism, has the effect of sustaining the dominant classes and weakening the challenges of those who wish to translate the concept of nationalism into an economic and social reality.

Of the two levels at which nationalism operates, the material level happens to be exclusive and accommodates less people than does the level of ideology the capacity of which to attract people is restricted by incredulity or apathy alone. The material level also generates tensions and stresses as more and more people try to acquire a footing on this very level. Those already there try to contain the exodus by, *inter alia,* making the level of ideology appear as attractive as possible. Promises and shibboleths are reinforced to ward off the eventuality of recourse to force. Nationalism, an instrument of change in the earlier colonial setting, becomes the handmaid of *status quo.* Nationalism liberates man only to hold him in bondage.

It is this consequence of his concentration on consensus as represented by ideology that the Indian historian of today has to recognise. Unless he has deliberately chosen to side with and promote the *status quo*, he is duty bound to work out in detail, from the point of view of the wretched and the miserable of his own brethren, the implications of consensus and to bring to light such conflict as it suits the dominant groups to keep hidden or diffused. This duty he owes not only to his social commitment to justice and equality as operative terms rather than as mere shibboleths; this also is a duty that is incumbent on him as a result of the demands of objectivity that his discipline imposes on him.

Nationalism, for too long, has been abused by the few. Historians may contribute to making it a liberating force once again. As for the ruling groups that may hinder this process, the warning may be offered that nationalism as the universally recognised principle of political integration subsumes within it both fusion and fission.

References

1. The best example of this is undoubtedly Bipan Chandra, *The Rise and Growth of Economic Nationalism in India : Economic Policies of Indian National Leadership?, 1880-1905,* New Delhi, 1966. Another example of marxian scholars succumbing to the tendency to highlight the emotional as the real *vis-a-vis* the material factor is provided by Sukhbir Choudhary, *Growth of Nationalism in India (1857-1918),* New Delhi, 1973 ; see particularly the Preface, pp. xii-xiii.
2. Ibid.,
3. Three works, revealing different intellectual orientations, may be cited as examples : Robin Jeffrey, *The Decline of Nayar Dominance : Society and Politics in Travancore, 1847-1908,* New Delhi, 1976; Sudhir Chandra, *Dependence and Disillusionment : Emergence of National Consciousness in Later 19th Century India,* New Delhi, 1975; Sumit Sarkar, *The Swadeshi Movement in Bengal 1903-1908,* New Delhi, 1973.

side with and [illegible] the masses [illegible] due, [illegible] were [illegible] from the point of view of [illegible] and [illegible] of [illegible] conservatives and [illegible] such slogans [illegible] results the dominant groups [illegible] The duty the [illegible] in order to justice and equality [illegible] than an [illegible] this also [illegible] as a result of the demands of [illegible] on him.

Nationalism [illegible] has been [illegible] by the [illegible] historians [illegible] making [illegible] for those [illegible] the [illegible] greater this process, the [illegible] may be [illegible] the [illegible] legislation [illegible] partition and fission.

References

1. [illegible]
2. Ibid.
3. [illegible]

Seven

CONFLICT AND CONSENSUS IN THE MAKING OF INDIA'S CONSTITUTION, 1946-50

PANCHANAND MISRA

THE MAKING of India's Constitution by the Constituent Assembly of India is a remarkable illustration of conflict and consensus in Indian society. The Constituent Assembly was boycotted by the Muslim league as it made a demand for Pakistan. The Native States of India also did not join. Pakistan was ultimately conceded but the League's representatives in India joined the Constituent Assembly. Even the nominees of the native states joined. Although the Congress had dominated the Constituent Assembly but prominent leaders of other political parties were accomodated. Mention may be made of B.R. Ambedkar, K.T. Shah, Shibban Lal Saksena and others. Even Jai Prakash Narayan was invited although he declined. The composition of the Constituent Assembly was broad-based; it included almost all the political parties of India except the Communist party. It represented all castes and creeds, all religions and sects and all the important communities of India.

The Constituent Assembly was conscious of its limitations as it was not directly elected by the people on the basis of adult suffrage. Therefore a questionnaire was prepared and circulated to the public for their comments. The Draft constitution was also circulated and a large number of amendments were received. Jai Prakash Narayan was one of those who had submitted amendments. These were examined by a special committee and some of them were accepted.

The working of the Constituent Assembly of India was also based on consensus rather than on the basis of majority voting. The Drafting Committee, therefore, consisted of all categories of members. B.R. Ambedkar was the chairman of the Committee. Sadulla of the Muslim league was also one of the members. This committee was elected unanimously. There was no party whip in this Congress-dominated House and the directives of Nehru and Patel were also turned down. Amendments moved by representatives of Minority parties were accepted. The desire of Rajendra Prasad, its chairman, to base the constitutional structure on village panchayat was turned down at the opposition of B.R. Ambedkar, though it was provided in the Directive Principles of State Policy. Thus, a large number of articles of the Draft constitution were scrapped and new amendments based on consensus were accepted. The language problem was also dealt with on the basis of consensus.

The constitution as such is based on the consensus of the people of India. The Sovereign Democratic Republic of India could find a place for the Raj-pramukhs. The Sovereign Democratic Republic of India could also be a member of the British Commonwealth of Nations. Consensus is the vitality of the Indian constitution. It is thus, that it has contained the communists and the DMIC, has survived two wars, and has outlived the emergency and the J.P. Movement at the same time.

ANCIENT TERMS AND MODERN CONNOTATIONS

Eight

THE BRAHMANA IN EARLY BUDDHISM

UMA CHAKRAVARTI

A STRIKING feature of the Buddhist *Vinaya Pitaka* in particular and the early Pali texts, in general, is the recurrence of certain terms, the meaning of which very frequently appears, at least at first instance, to be unrelated to the passage in question, or even seems to have been used in a contradictory manner at different points in the texts. These terms and what they represent have not always been explained adequately and this has led to a certain lacuna in our understanding of them. However, if one views the texts as a system, a unified whole, with an intrinsic logic, and relates this to the specific situational context in which they occur one may be able to arrive at a more satisfactory comprehension of the terms used. In this paper I shall be concerned with only one of them : the term Brahmana.

An analysis of the situations in which the term Brahmana occurs in the Pali texts suggests that the apparent contradiction noticeable at first instance, actually has a pattern which is discernible on closer examination. There are a large number of references on the Brahmanas as upholders of the existing ritual system, or to their pride in their inherent superior status in the social hierarchy, and of these the Pali texts are extremely critical. In all these contexts the Buddhists see themselves in opposition to the

Brahmanas and make derogatory references to them. The Brahmanas here are viewed as a social category claiming religious and social preeminence as an inherent right. The Buddhists as part of the wider *parivrajáka* or *sramana* tradition were dissidents and they were in their general attitude anti-Vedic and anti-Brahmanic[1]. The heretical sects were opposed to the more ancient tradition of the Brahmanas especially to the latter's claim to a special knowledge of the revealed teaching, hereditary in their caste.[2] At the root of this opposition lay the fact that the Brahmana was seen as a householder, and therefore the Buddhist monk who had renounced the material world and the Brahmana householder were polar opposites. The *sramana* or *parivrajaka* broke especially those rules that applied to the householder. The Buddhist monks were discredited by the Brahmanas for having renounced social life and duties prematurely. The Buddha himself was abused for this by a Brahmana householder at Savatthi[3]. The Buddha also repeatedly rejected the Brahmanas' claim to supremacy based on inherent characteristics. In a very revealing passage[4] the Buddha is critical of a Brahmana priest teaching a *mantra* to a king seated on a high seat, while he himself sat on a low seat, thereby falling from the ideal of a religious teacher or a spiritually elevated person. Buddha exhorts him to "go forth" (*i.e.* from the home). This statement is particularly important because it focuses on the root of the opposition between the Sramana and the Brahmana : the condition of homelessness. In this connection the grammarian Patanjali's use of the term *Sramanabrahmana* to illustrate an antagonistic compound is very significant. He remarks that the opposition of the two was eternal, like that of the snake and the mongoose.[5]

On the other hand the Pali texts have numerous references to the term Brahmana where they are seen as possessors of spirituality in conjunction with the Sramana. It is in this sense that the term *Sramanabrahmana* appears in the Pali literature of the Buddhists. While the Sramana and the Brahmana are quite clearly two distinct and opposing categories, jointly they are seen as a respected group, in opposition to the mass of people. Here the term

Brahmana appears in the sense of the ideal value of spirituality as an acquired characteristic. The Buddha, it should be remembered, while attacking the Brahmana, did not reject the term Brahmana as a conceptual category. He redefined it as is evident from the Brahmanavagga in the *Dhammapada*, where it is very clear that the ideal Brahmana is the Buddha. The Buddhists associate themselves with the Brahmana in contexts where the term Brahmana is being used in the sense of a value.

It will be apparent from the brief discussion above that the meaning of the term Brahmana is not constant; it is, in linguistic vocabulary, a 'shifter'. It shifts according to the context but always along two axes : social category and ideal value. As V. Das has shown in the context of medieval Hinduism[6], it is in fact a 'mediating category' and mediates between two polar opposites : the social and the asocial. The term Brahmana in Pali literature appears, on the one hand, to have been attributed characteristics similar to the Sramana, and on the other with characteristics as opposed to it. The Buddhists adopt a stand of opposition as well as unity to the term Brahmana. As a social category with inherent rights they challenge their authority and are opposed to them, but as a term of 'value' and as possessors of spirituality as an acquired characteristic, they are in unity.

References

1. B.M. Barua, *Pre-Buddhist Indian Philosophy*, Delhi, 1970.
2. A.K. Warder, "On the Relationship between Buddhism and Other Contemporary Systems." *BSOAS*, Vol. XVIII, 1956 : pp. 43-63.
3. *Samyutta Nikaya*, 1. p.162.
4. *The Book of Discipline* (translated by I.B. Horner), Vol. III, London, 1942, p. 148.
5. *Vyakarana Mahabhashyam*, 2.4.9, Vol. II, p. 853.
6. V. Das, *Structure and Cognition*, Oxford University Press, Delhi, 1977,pp. 46-47

Brahmana as an inferior in the sense of the ideal value of spirituality [illegible] and good character. The Buddha, it should be [illegible] [illegible] Brahmana, did not reject the [illegible] Brahmana as a social category he redeemed [illegible] is evident from the [illegible] in the *Dhammapada* [illegible]. It is very clear that the ideal Brahmana is the Buddha. The Buddhists associate themselves with the Brahmana in contexts where the term Brahmana is being used in the sense of a value.

It will thus appear from the brief discussion above that the meaning of the term Brahmana is not constant. It is, in linguistic vocabulary, a [illegible]. It shifts according to the context, but always [illegible] two axes: social category and ideal value. [illegible] has shown in the context of medieval [illegible] that [illegible] a mediating category and mediates between two polar opposites: the [illegible] and the ascetic. The term Brahmana in Pali literature appears, on the one hand, to have been attributed characteristics similar to the [illegible] and on the other with characteristics as opposed to it. The Buddhists are in a state of opposition as well as unity towards Brahmana. As a social category with immense [illegible] they challenge their authority and are opposed to them, but as [illegible] of value and as possessors of spirituality and [illegible] characteristics, they are in unity.

References

1. [illegible], Delhi, 1970.
2. A.K. Warder, [illegible] Buddhism and Other [illegible], BSOAS, Vol. XVIII, 1956, pp. [illegible]
3. [illegible], 1972.
4. *The Book of the Discipline* translated by I.B. Horner, Vol. [illegible], London, [illegible], p. [illegible]
5. [illegible] Vol. II, p. 381.
6. V. Das, *Structure and Cognition*, Oxford University Press, Delhi, 1977, pp. [illegible]

Nine

SOME ANCIENT TERMS AND THEIR CONNOTATIONS IN THE ARTHASASTRA OF KAUTILYA

PANDEY

THE ARTHASASTRA of Kautilya has universally been accepted as a monumental source of ancient Indian history, culture and polity. But what has not been adequately appreciated by scholars is its great value in revealing the meaning and connotations of a large number of technical words used in our literature and inscriptions. Here are a few examples to illustrate this point :

1. The sixth line of the Jaunpur Inscription[1] of Isvaravarman reads as follows :

Dhara-margga-vinirgatagni-kanika

According to Fleet, it means 'a spark of fire that had come by the road from (the city of) Dhara'.[2]

Sudhakar Chattopadhyaya has also accepted this interpretation.

Disagreeing with these scholars, Basak has observed that 'in all likelihood the word *dhara* refers to the edge of a sword used by the Maukhari king(?) from which sparks of fire came out'.[3]

D.C. Sircar has interpreted *'dhara-marga'* as 'the passage of the (hero's) sword' and has offered the following explanation for his interpretation :

"Fleet's interpretation of the passage is clearly wrong. In the first place, 'a spark of fire that had come by the road from Dhara does not appear to offer a good sense.

Secondly, the city of Dhara seems to have been built by the Paramaras, and it is hardly possible that it existed much earlier than the age of the Paramara king Bhoja I, (c. 1000-1055 A.D.)' ".[4]

But from the *Arthasastra* of Kautilya it appears that the words *'dhara-marga'* had a technical meaning. Thus, *'Vikramo bhadrasvaso, bharavahya iti margah. Vikramo valgitamupa-kanthamupajavo javascha dharah'*.[5]

Here, the words *'dhara'* and *'marga'* meant 'gait' and 'speed' of the horse, respectively. That the word *'dhara'* was actually used in this sense even later is borne out by *the Sisupalavadham*.[6]

Therefore, the expression *'Dhara-marga-vinirgatagnikanika'* should mean 'the sparks of fire coming from (the hooves of horses of) different speed and gait'. It denotes a military operation remarkable for the swift action of its cavalry.

2. Speaking about the retreat of the Indo-Greeks from Madhyadesa, the *Yuga Purana*, V. 7, says :

> *Madhyadese na sthasyanti yavana yuddhadurmadah Tesam anyonya sambhavah bhavisyanti na samsayah Atmachakrotthitam ghoram yuddham paramadarunam.*

Here, the words *'sambhavah'* and *'atmachakrotthitam'* have been translated differently by scholars. H.C. Raychaudhuri[7] translates the *sloka* as follows :

> 'The fiercely fighting Greeks will not stay in the Madhyadesa, there will be a cruel, dreadful war *in their own kingdom, caused between themselves*'. Though, he has translated the word, *'anyonya-sambhavah'* as 'caused between themselves', he places a question mark after it to convey his doubt.

D.C. Sircar[8] thinks that *'anyonya-sambhavah'* and *'atmachakrotthitam'* should mean 'internal dissensions' and 'in their own kingdom', respectively.

According to K.A.N. Sastri[9], the whole sloka should be translated as follows :

> 'The Yavanas, furious in battle, will not stay in the Middle country, there will be, without doubt, *mutual conflicts; out of their own circles* will arise an awful and supremely lamentable strife'.

Sudhakar Chattopadhyaya[10] offers the following translation :

> 'The Yavanas, intoxicated with fighting, will not stay in 'the Madhyadesa': there will be undoubtedly *a civil war* among them; *arising in their own country*, there will be a very terrible and ferocious war.'

It appears that the word '*sambhavah*' occuring in the *Yuga Purana* was intelligible not even to most ancient editors with the result that it was replaced by '*samgramah*' in some copies.

However, a perusal of the *Arthasastra* of Kautilya indicates that the word '*sambhava*' neither meant 'caused' (Raychaudhuri) nor 'dissensions' (Sircar) nor 'conflict' (Sastri) nor 'a civil war' (Chattopadhyaya). According to the '*Arthasastra*' '*atma-sambhavito*' clearly means 'self-conceited'.[11] '*Sambhava*', thus, should be taken to mean 'conceit'. The author of the *Yuga Purana* is referring to the self-conceit of the Greek princes which gave rise to strife and brought about their downfall.

The expression '*atma-chakrotthitam*' has generally been interpreted as 'in their own kingdom', 'out of their own circles' or 'arising in their own country'.

However, the *Arthasastra* of Kautilya[12] suggests a different meaning. Its use of the term '*para-chakra*' gives us the clue to the meaning of *atma-chakra* :

Para-chakratavigrastam vyadhidurbhikshapiditam
Desam pariharet raja vyaya-kridascha varayet.

It is obvious that in '*para-chakratavigrastam desam*' the word '*desa*' means a kingdom, a territory. '*Chakra*' must mean something else. If we take it to mean 'circle', '*para-chakra*' should be interpreted as 'circle of enemies'. Conversely, the expression '*atma-chakra*' should be interpreted as 'one's own circle'. '*Atma-chakrotthitam yuddham*' mentioned in the *Yuga-Purana* would, therefore, mean a civil war caused by members of one and the same ruling circle.

3. The Junagarh Inscription claims that during the reign of Skandagupta, there were no 'kadarya' in his kingdom.[13] This word again has a technical meaning the significance of which has not been properly understood.

Kautilya has defined a '*kadarya*' in the following words :
'*yo bhrtyatmapidabhyamupachinotyartham sa kadaryah*'[14]
('Whoever hoards money, entailing hardship both on himself and his servants, is a *kadarya*').

4. The Allahabad Pillar Inscription of Samudragupta contains the following line :

atma-nivedana-kanyopayana-dana... etc.

Raychaudhuri[15] has translated this line as 'offer of personal service, bringing of gifts of maidens. . .' etc.

According to R. C. Majumdar, *atma-nivedana* means 'literally' offering oneself as sacrifice, or, probably means personal attendance, whereas '*kanyopayana-dana*' means 'presenting unmarried daughters and giving them in marriage'.[16]

Sudhakar Chattopadhyaya's view is similar to that of Raychaudhuri. According to him, *atma-nivedana* means 'offering their own persons for service to the emperor'. As regards '*kanyopayana-dana*', he has translated it as 'gifts of maidens'.

It appears that the term '*atma-nivedana*' is synonymous with Kautilya's '*atmopanidhana*' which he explains in the following manner :

'*Yoham Sa bhavanyanmama dravyam tatbhavata svakrtyeshu prayojyatamityatmopanidhanamiti*'[17].

(To say, 'What I am, that thou art; thou mayest utilise in thy works whatever is mine', is identity of interest-*atmopanidhanam*).

As regards '*kanyopayana-dana*', it has not been explained properly because of the arbitrary jumbling up of two different technical terms—'*kanyopayana*' and '*dana*'. '*Kanyopayana*' certainly means 'giving daughters in marriage'. This act constituted what was known as *kanya-samdhi* in ancient India. But if we combine the word '*kanyopayana*' with '*dana*' and interpret it as 'presenting unmarried daughters' and 'giving them in marriage', there is a clumsy duplication. To quote R.C. Majumdar, 'it is not easy to distinguish between the two (namely, presenting unmarried daughters and giving them in marriage). For it would be unreasonable to think that rulers who enjoyed at least some degree of autonomy would present their daughters for any other purpose than marriage.'[18]

In fact, the word '*dana*' in the Allahabad Pillar Inscription has been used in a specific sense and it constituted another act of homage to the emperor on the part of the subordinate kings. It is synonymous with Kautilya's '*upapradana*' which he explains in the following manner :

upapradanamarthopakarah[19]

(Doing financial good is *upapradana*).

5. There is a good deal of controversy as to whether '*ayas*' or '*kalayas*' used in the *Rgveda* actually meant 'iron'. To quote V.M. Apte,[20] 'What metal the *ayas* was is uncertain. It may have been either copper, bronze or iron...'. But Kautilya clearly regards *kalayas* as iron distinguished from copper, bronze, brass and other alloys. To quote him,[21] '*kalayasatamravrttakamsyasisatrapuvaikrntakarakutani lohani*'. This was probably the case in the Rgvedic age also.

References

1. *CII* Vol. III, pp. 228 ff.
2. Ibid., p. 230.
3. *History of North-East India,* p. 129.
4. *JIH* Vol. XLII Part I, *April, 1964,* p. 130.
5. *Artha.,* 2.30.45-46, *Vikramo bhadrasvaso bharavahya iti margah, Vikramo valgitamupakanthamupajavo javascha dharah.*
6. *Sisupalavadham* 5.60, *Dhara prasadhayitu-mavyatikunarupah.*
7. *PHAI,* p. 386.
8. *The Age of Imperial Unity,* p. 107.
9. *A Comp. Hist. of India,* Vol. II, p. 156.
10. *E.H.N.I.*, p. 8.
11. Atmasambhavitah ... tikshnah, sahasikah bhogena samtushtah-iti manivargah. *Artha.* 1.14.5.
12. Ibid., 2.1.36.
13. Tasmin nrpe sasati naiva kaschit dharmadapeto manujah prajasu arto daridro vyasani kadarya dandyo na va yo bhrsapiditah syat.
14. *Artha.* 2.9.23.
15. *PHAI,* p. 546.
16. *VGA,* p. 148.
17. *Artha.* 2.10.53.
18. *VGA,* p. 148.
19. *Artha.* 2.10.54.
20. *V.A.*, p. 397.
21. *Artha.* 2.17.14.

Ten

BHAKTI

KRISHNA SHARMA

BHAKTI IS a general term, but it has acquired a specific definition and technical meaning in modern scholarship, which is both artificial and erroneous. The existing academic definition of bhakti is a recent phenomenon; it is not corroborated by Hindu religious texts, not even those which are usually cited to support it[1]. It is a direct product of the theorisation on the Bhakti theme by certain Western Indologists of the 19th century and was shaped by their alien standards of judgement. Its main architects were : H.H. Wilson, Albrecht Weber, Monier-Williams, and George Grierson. Since the theories propounded by them have not been questioned till now, a faulty definition of bhakti cotinues to be in usage in Indian studies, historical as well as others. As it has served as the main guideline for all assessments and analyses of the medieval religious developments, collectively known as the Bhakti-Movement, it needs rectification in historical writings.

The current theories about bhakti describe it as a religion and a cult; they also define and analyse it as a doctrine and a theology[2]. According to the views that prevail in academic circles today, bhakti is understood as a monotheism based on the belief in a personal God and in the fundamental dualism between God and man. Consequently, it is interpreted as an antithesis of the monistic content of Hinduism and the belief in an impersonal concept of God that goes with it. In other words, it is taken as the opposite pole of the nirguna ideology of the Upanishads and that of the Advaita Vedanta. Theorisation about bhakti on these lines is also accompanied with the idea that the path of bhakti is opposed to the path of jnana; and that the one is the converse of the other. Besides, bhakti has got more or less identified with Vaishnavism in modern academic works[3]. Consequently, it is studied and explained mainly from a Vaishnava viewpoint, so much so that the studies of bhakti have often turned out to be studies of Vaishnavism and *vice-a-versa*. These postulations about bhakti and its identification with Vaishnavism, however, ignore the generic meaning of the term bhakti itself. They also overlook its full implications in the total context of the Hindu religious tradition.

The word bhakti is derived from the root *bhaj* by adding the suffix *ktin* (ti). The suffix *ktin* is usually added to a verb to form an action or agent noun[4]. Bhakti (bhaj+ti), according to the rules of Panini indicates a *bhava* or condition[5]. The root *bhaj* however can be used in any of the following meanings :

> to partake of, to resort to, to declare for, to pursue, to prefer or choose, to serve and honour, to love and adore.

Bhakti, therefore, denotes participation as well as experience, recourse as well as cultivation, and reverence as well as adoration. Evidently, it is a general and relative term which can be used in any of the above meanings in a wide range of contexts, the object of bhakti remaining a variable factor. That is, it can assume particularity only when it is viewed in relation with the object towards which it is directed. Taken in the religious context, in which this term is generally used, it can mean devotion to God only in a general sense. By itself it cannot suggest any individual religious mode, nor can it imply any doctrinaire or ideational position. Its nature and expression in a particular religious tradition, therefore, is conditioned by the nature of the cognition of God found therein, and the beliefs and practices connected therewith. The initial acceptance of bhakti as a religion and a cult is in itself a mistake; to explain it as a doctrine and theology is equally misleading. The Hindus never used the term bhakti to denote any religion (*dharma*) or religious sect (*sampradaya).* Nor did they use it for any doctrine (*siddhanta)* or school of thought (*mata)*[6]. The view that bhakti is incompatible with the Advaita Vedanta is also a fallacy. When bhakti is discussed in relation with the Advaita Vedanta of Sankaracharya, the former is described as theism, and the latter, as pure philosophy. This amounts to a denial of the religious significance of a very vital aspect of Hinduism. The advaita vedanta can hardly be brushed aside as non-religious and non-devotional. Significantly enough, Sankaracharya himself speaks of bhakti in his *Viveka-Chudamani,* where he describes it as *jnana-nishtha*[7]. The juxtaposition of bhakti and jnana is also unwarranted. The two appear as perfectly compatible and inclusive of each other in most of the Hindu religious texts, including those which are quoted in modern academic works to maintain the difference between bhakti and jnana[8]. The identification of bhakti with Vaishnavism and its interpretation in the light of Vaishnava beliefs and practices is also an error since it amounts to taking an extremely restricted view of bhakti.

In so far as the different denominations of the Hindus conceive God in different forms, personal as well as impersonal, bhakti in the general sense of devotion, remains common to all. However, variations can be caused in its nature and overt expressions on account of the pluralistic character of the Hindu religious tradition from the standpoint of faith, ideas, and practices. Hence the expressions, Vishnu-bhakti, Krishna-bhakti, Siva-bhakti etc., and also the categories, saguna-bhakti and nirguna-bhakti. The standardized definition of bhakti which is being questioned here meets the specifications of saguna-bhakti only, and that too, mainly from the Vaishnava angle. It is totally at variance with the tradition of nirguna bhakti and delimits its correct comprehension and assessment. It would be relevant to state here, that this has led to an outstanding academic ambivalence in the studies of the medieval Bhakti-Movement in particular. The monolithic view of the movement in the light of the present definition of bhakti has led to the established practice of co-relating the nirguna and saguna bhaktas in spite of their fundamental ideological differences. The historical perspective used to fix the source of inspiration of all medieval bhaktas to Ramanujacharya, Nimbarka, Madhva and Vallabhacharya and their systems of Vedanta is also due to the same reason. An important fact is altogether ignored; namely, that the ideology of the aforesaid acharyas, all of whom were Vaishnavas and the protagonists of Saguna bhakti is not borne out by all the medieval bhaktas. This inconsistency prevails entirely because of not taking cognizance of the generic meaning of the term bhakti.

The misrepresentation of the term bhakti, and the concurrent fallacies were not the result of a mere semantic error. Ignoring the Hindu testimony available, the bhakti theories were contrived by the western scholars with the aid of their own measures of judgement, regardless of their inapplicability to Hinduism. They were mainly two. One, the principle of division and distinction between religion and philosophy; and two, the dictum that theistic religions are only those based on the belief in a personal God. A corollary of these was the principle of differentiation between monotheism and monism according to which belief in one 'personal' God alone could be adjudged as monotheism, and the belief in the oneness of an impersonal God had to be set aside as monism.

The spurious nature of the present definition of bhakti, and the supporting theories which go with it, becomes all the more evident when the entire process of their formation is taken into account. Their origins can be traced back to the latter half of the 19th century, and their fuller formation to its last quarter. They had assumed a fixed character and were generally current by the end of it. The earlier western observers who wrote about Hinduism[9] at the end of the 18th and during the first half of the 19th century did not mention any bhakti cult or religion. Nor did they underline Vaishnavism as a form of monotheism. On the contrary, they showed a tendency to accept Hindu monotheism on its own terms and saw nothing more in

Vaishnavism than the worship of 'deified heroes' Rama and Krishna[10]. But the works written during the latter half of the 19th century show an altogether different trend. The gradual and laboured process through which the bhakti theories were evolved during this period is fully traceable. A survey of the sequence of opinions of the authors responsible for their formulation can further reveal their artificial nature.

It was H.H. Wilson who first mentioned bhakti as a religion in his handbook on the *Religious Sects of the Hindus*, published in 1846. He did so in connection with the Vaishnavas of Bengal and stated that 'their religion' can be summed up in one word, 'bhakti'[11]. He was obviously referring to the followers of Chaitanya and the Gaudiya School of Vaishnavism which lays an exclusive emphasis on Krishna-bhakti. Wilson did not define bhakti any further. In fact, he did not even connect it with Vaishnavism as a whole. While listing twenty sects of the Vaishnavas, he had mentioned bhakti only in relation to the Vaishnava Goswamis of Bengal[12]. But since Wilson's *Religious Sects of the Hindus* was the first standard work of its kind, the initial reference to bhakti in it in connection with the Krishna-cult, had a far reaching effect. Soon the two got identified with each other in the contemporary circle of western Indologists.

Albrecht Weber developed the bhakti theme further in his paper on *Uber die Krishnajanmashtami* delivered to *Akademic der Wissenschaften* in 1867. He wrote on bhakti, in the sense of the Krishna-cult of course, mainly to point out the similarities between Krishna-worship and Christianity. Whereas Wilson had said too little about bhakti in conceptual terms, Weber treated it almost as a doctrine and explained it as a theology. Furthermore, he described bhakti as a monotheism, and as an emotional religion of fervent faith[13]. Soon the idea gained ground that the 'bhakti religion' was the Hindu theistic expression comparable with the Christian theism. After Wilson, it was Weber who contributed the most in preparing the groundwork for the bhakti theories. In fact, his writings paved the way for the subsequent growth of academic opinion on the subject. Auguste Barth, a contemporary of Weber had rightly stated that the bhakti theory "in its scientific form belongs entirely to Professor Weber and which that scholar has developed from time to time .."[14].

The ideas initially launched by Wilson and Weber were strengthened most by Monier-Williams through his more systematic and scholarly expositions. His works *Indian Wisdom* and *Brahmanism and Hinduism* published in 1875 and 1891 need special mention in this connection. Unlike Wilson and Weber, Monier Williams did not confine bhakti to the Krishna-cult; he related it with the whole of Vaishnavism. Going in for a broader study of Hinduism, and making use of the western conceptual categories of theism, pantheism and monotheism with greater acumen, he went ahead to theorise on Vaishnavism, and thereby, on bhakti. Monier Williams described Vaishnavism as the only Hindu system worthy of being called a religion[15]. He argued, 'there can be no true religion without a personal devotion to a personal God...'[16]. Arguing on these lines, he stated that Vaishnavism alone had the true ingredients of 'monotheism', since it is characterised by the 'abolition of the triune equality of Brahma, Siva and Vishnu in favour of Vishnu...'[17]. The idea that bhakti, jnana, and karma are separate paths, exclusive of each other, can be traced back to the writings of Sir Monier-Williams. Concentrating on the personal image of God in Vaishnavism and the 'religion of bhakti', he said, 'who can doubt that a God of such a character was needed, a God who could satisfy the yearnings of the heart for a religion of faith, love and prayer rather than of knowledge (jnana) and works (karma). Such a God was believed to be represented by Vishnu'[18]. Similarly, he projected the idea that bhakti represents a position opposite to that of Advaita Vedanta. He was able to do so more effectively than Wilson and Weber by drawing a dividing line between what he called 'Brahmanism' and 'Hinduism'; he listed Vaishnavism under the latter category. That made it easier for him to set aside the Advaita Vedanta as a Brahmanical 'intellectual pantheism', different from the monotheism of the Vaishnavas and their religion of bhakti.

The element of contrivance in Monier-Williams' theorisation is quite evident. In his earlier writings he had acknowledged that even "the most profound forms of Indian pantheism rest on the fundamental doctrine of God's unity" and that even the ordinary Hindu, who practises the most corrupt form of polytheism is never found to deny the doctrine of God's unity"[19]. The works of his later years carry a very different strain.

The theories propounded by the aforesaid authors were finally bound together in a neat system by George Grierson. He presented a more integrated and definitive account of bhakti as a religion. Whatever Wilson had said about the Krishna-cult, and Monier-Williams, about Vaishnavism was now defined by him as the Bhakti-Religion in a general sense. He described it as the 'devoted faith directed to a personal God'[20] and as the 'monotheistic religion of ancient India'[21] which had existed 'in contradistinction to the pantheistic Brahmanism'[22] and was strongly opposed to the 'Advaita Vedantist doctrine of Salvation by knowledge..'[23]. He also took a leap forward by constructing a continuous account of the Bhakti Religion (as conceived in western scholarship), from the ancient to the medieval period of Indian history, and added yet another dimension to the bhakti theories by concentrating on the medieval bhaktas.[24] If they were all bhaktas and spoke of bhakti, a common ideology could be attributed to them all in the light of what was being defined as bhakti in the west. In short the bhakti theories were crystallised and were established more firmly through the writings of George Grierson. Their roots had grown deep by 1909 when Bhakti was incorporated in the Encyclopedia of Religion and Ethics as a religion and doctrine, fully equipped with all its present technical implications[25].

It did not prove difficult for the above ideas to get deeply entrenched in Indian scholarship. The reasons are simple to explain. All academic studies of Indian themes on modern historical—analytical lines were undertaken first by western Indologists The new class of Indian scholars of the ninteenth century, with western education and modern academic training, had inevitably to fall back on the relevant frames of reference already worked out in western writings. As in many other fields of scholarship, in the study of Hinduism also, the initial framework provided by western scholarship could not be dispensed with easily. The early modern India scholars, therefore, had to work with an already established definition of bhakti. They could not avoid the identification of Krishna-worship and Vaishnavism in their writings. Nor could they question the hypothesis that bhakti was a specific 'monotheistic' religious tradition different from the monism or pantheism of the Upanishads and the Advaita Vedanta.

R.G. Bhandarkar, a contemporary of Weber, Monier-Williams and Grierson, deserves special attention in this connection, since he was the first Indian to write on the bhakti theme on modern academic lines. Bhandarkar had devoted his entire attention to one thing, *i.e.* to refute the theories that had been advanced by Weber and others to prove the influence of Christianity on bhakti. His main purpose was to establish the indigenous nature of what had been termed as the Bhakti religion by western scholars. Accepting Weber's identification of bhakti with the Krishna-cult, he went ahead to establish its nature, character and antiquity with the support of eprigraphic and literary evidence to show its existence in the pre-Christian era[26]. The scholarly contributions of Bhandarkar had no doubt laid the question of the Christian influence on bhakti at rest. But since he had not questioned the identification of bhakti with Krishna-worship, his attempts to establish its antiquity had in fact established the antiquity of Vaishnavism and the cult of Krishna-Vasudeva only. Bhandarkar had not only accepted the term bhakti in a restricted sense, he had also accepted it as a designation for Hindu monotheism. He had also recognized the principle that bhakti and monotheism could be possible only in relation to a personal God, and therefore, continued to speak of Hindu monotheism in terms of the Krishna cult and Vaishnavism. In other words, Bhandarkar did not examine the full implications of the term bhakti as used in the Hindu religious texts. Nor did he attempt an independent analysis of the nature of Hindu monotheism which had been identified with it. This oversight on the part of a man of his erudition at a time when two of his contemporaries (Monier Williams and George Grierson) were busy giving a final shape to the bhakti theories made their task easier. In fact, this indirect support from an Indian scholar strengthened the base for the further study of bhakti on the established lines.[27] Thus, in so far as Bhandarkar did not question the artificial definition of bhakti, he was responsible, though unwillingly for the transference of the existing errors into Indian scholarship. A lot more has been written by Indian authors since the days of Bhandarkar on the bhakti theme, but without any effort for a fresh start to examine the basic errors involved in the academic definition of bhakti which has remained current, in academic circles for a hundred years and more.

The frame of reference provided by the misrepresentation of the term bhakti has led to a great deal of speculation about bhakti and the Bhakti-movement. A number of theories have been forwarded from time to time, all of which cannot be taken into account here. The most recent example, however, is of the use of bhakti to define the "concept and content of medievalism" in Indian history[28]. But every theorisation on bhakti and the Bhakti-movement, in so far as it rests on a faulty and artificial definition of bhakti, is bound to prove vulnerable. Much of what has been written till now about bhakti and the Bhakti-movement awaits a more serious and careful scrutiny by historians as well as scholars from other relevant disciplines.

References

1. The texts generally cited are the *Bhagavad-Gita,* the *Bhagvata Purana,* and the *Bhakti Sutras* of Narada and Sandilya.
2. Treating bhakti as a religion, cult, and doctrine is a general phenomenon in evidence in various disciplines. To cite a few clear examples in historical writing : R.C. Majumdar and Tarachand refer to it as a religion (R.C. Majumdar, *The History and Culture of the Indian People*, Vol. IV, 1960, p. 47; Tarachand, *Influence of Islam on Indian Culture,* 1936, pp. 25-26); Yusuf Hussain describes it as a culture "Islam and the cult of bhakti" (*in Glimpses of Medieval Indian Culture,* 1957; R.S. Sharma calls it a doctrine (The Indian Historical Review, March 1974, Vol I., Number I, p. 9).

3. See H.C. Raychaudhuri, *Materials for the Study of the Early History of the Vaishnava Sect, 1920*, p. 6.
4. Panini, *Ashtadhyayi*, III. 3.94.
5. Ibid., III. 3.18.
6. Significantly enough bhakti does not find any mention in the two well-known compendia of the different siddhantas, namely the *Sarva Siddhanta Sangraha* of Sankaracharya and the *Sarva Darsana Sangraha of Madhavacharya*.
7. jnananishtha para bhaktirityuchyate.
   Sankaracharya, *Gita Bhashya*, XVIII. 55.
8. The only exceptions are the works of the Goswamis of the Chaitanya school which do make a distinction between bhakti and jnana. But being works of minor significance, they are not cited. It is the Gita, the Bhagavata-Purana and the Bhakti-sutras that are generally used.
9. J.Z. Holwell, Charles Wilkins, H.T. Colebrooke, William Ward etc.
10. H.T. Colebrooke, *Miscellaneous Essays*, London, 1873, Vol. II, p. 211. William Ward, *A View of the History, Literature and Mythology of the Hindoos.*, London, 1822, Vol. I, p. LXXIV.
11. H.H. Wilson, *Sketch of the Religious Sects of the Hindus*, Bishop College Press, Calcutta, 1846, p. 100.
12. Ibid., pp. 100-102.
13. Albrecht Weber, *Uber die Krishna janmashtmi* (Krishna's Gebertsfest), Akademie Wissenschaften, Berlin, 1867, pp. 321 ff.
14. Auguste Barth, *The Religions of India*, Kegal Paul, London, 1906, p. 220.
15. Monier-Williams, *Brahmanism and Hinduism*, John Murray, London, 1891. p. 96.
16. Monier-Williams, "The Vaishnava Religion", in : *The Journal of the Royal Asiatic Society*, London, 1882, pp. 295-6.
17. Monier-Williams, "The Vaishnava Religion", *op. cit.* p.295.
18. Monier-Williams, *Brahmanism and Hinduism, op. cit.*, p. 97.
19. Monier-Williams, "Indian Theistic Reformers", *The Journal of Royal Asiatic Society*, London, 1881, p. 1.
20. G.A. Grierson, "The Modern Hindu Doctrine of Works", *JRAS*, 1908, p. 337.
21. George A. Grierson, *The Monotheistic Religion of Ancient India and its Descendant, the Modern Doctrine of Faith*, read at the Third International Congress for the History of Religions, held at Oxford in September, 1908.
22. G.A. Grierson, *Narayana and the Bhagavatas*, Reprinted from Indian Antiquary, British India Press, Bombay, 1909, p. 4.
23. G.A. Grierson, The Hindu Doctrine of Works, ibid., p. 337.
24. See Grierson's History of Hindi Literature.
25. *Encyclopedia of Religion and Ethics*, edited by James Hastings, 1909, Vol. II, pp. 539-551.
26. R.G. Bhandarkar, *Vaishnavism, Saivism and Minor Religious Systems*, J. Trubner, Strassburg, 1913, pp. 3, 4, 14, 29, **38**.

27. According to Grierson, the paper read by Bhandakar at the Vienna Oriental Congress in 1886 had opened the way for all subsequent researches on the subject.
    G.A. Grierson, *Journal of Royal Asiatic Society*, For The First Half Year of 1910, p. 172.
28. Professor R.S. Sharma lists bhakti as one of the major characteristics of Medievalism, along with others such as feudalism etc. He explains that "Bhakti reflected the complete dependence of the tenants or semi serfs on the landowners in the medieval times".
    R.S. Sharma, "Problem of Transition from Ancient to Medieval History", *The Indian Historical Review*, March, 1974, Vol. I, No. I., pp. 8-9.

PERIODIZATION

Eleven

THE CONCEPT OF THE GOLDEN AGE AND SOME GENERAL PROBLEMS

RASESH JAMINDAR

Meaning of History

LET US first make clear the meaning and scope of history. History is the outward expression of the human mind or thought. Ravindra Nath Tagore has rightly stated that "there is only one History—The History of Man". Closely interwoven with the problem of definition is the question of its scope. History, is not a mere catalogue of political events but includes in its fold the achievements of the common people in every walk of life. It is an account of the social and cultural growth and development of a people.

History means "any kind of inquiry in the field of human past. It is, therefore not limited to what is ordinarily taught as history, but includes the history of art, language, literature, institutions, science, religion, philosophy, literacy, textual and aesthetic criticism, interpretation of work and movements, research of artistic, poetical, political and religious forms, their first appearances, their weathering away and their rekindling". (Daedalus, Spring, 1970, p. 241).

Periodisation

Historians have divided our history into three periods

viz., ancient, medieval and modern on the basis of the advent of Hindus, Muslims and Europeans, overlooking the basic fact that history is an everflowing continuous stream of human activities. Moreover, it is not true that during Hindu India the rulers were all Hindus. There were also Buddhist and Jaina kings, such as Asoka, Kharvela, Kanishka and Harsha. Generally we close the ancient period with the death of Harsha. What do we do with the centuries between Harsha's death and the foundation of Muslim rule in India identified with the medieval period? If we label the medieval period as Muslim, the Rajput and other Hindu states have to be accounted for. As for the British period there were Hindu as well as Muslim princely states.

Is modernity a characteristic of the modern period? Was the 'modern period' society as catholic in nature and secular in outlook as Aryan Society of the ancient times? The people of the Harappan civilization were enjoying the advantages of a drainage system as early as 3rd millenium B.C. The towns and cities of 'modern' India were not—are still not-equipped with this bare amenity? 'Modern' society can be designated as traditional in many ways and ancient society as modern. Thus, neither the concepts ancient, medieval and modern nor Hindu, Muslim and British are satisfactory for the periodisation of Indian history.

Perhaps we should classify our history as past history and present history or early history and contemporary history. Further it would be desirable to classify political history on the basis of political events and royal dynasties and genealogies; religious history on the basis of religious movements, art history on the basis of art styles and so on and so forth.

Concept of Golden Age

We also need to reappraise the concept of Golden age. When a particular period witnesses prosperity in every sphere of human life we designate it as the Golden Age. Moreover we attribute the prosperity to the ruling king or a dynasty. Is it logical to do so? Is progress an overnight business? Is it not the result of the labour of a number of people over a long period of time covered by a number of dynasties? We should not fail to put on record the work done by earlier generations of people and their rulers. In fact, they deserve the real credit for achievements which become manifest later.

The term golden age should signify freedom from the worry of external aggression or internal conflict, absence of state interference in the day to day life of the people, availability of household commodities at reasonable prices, state patronage for social and cultural enterprises, devotion on the part of the rulers to the welfare of the people, economic progress and stability, social and economic equality amongst all creeds, classes, and colours of people, a state of peace, and, most importantly, a people inspired to work for their all round development. According to this definition can we describe the Gupta and Mughal periods as the Golden ages of Indian History?

Interdisciplinary Approach

In addition to the specific and thorough knowledge of one discipline, it is necessary to have a reasonable degree of acquaintance with other disciplines. This is a prerequisite for effective research. The political historian, the social historian, the religious historian, the economic historian, and the art historian have to work together to achieve best results in the reappraisal of history.

Regional Histories

There is an urgent need to write local histories in a vast country like ours. This will facilitate the task of writing a comprehensive history of the nation. As the sources for local history are often in regional languages, they should be written by local people who know these languages well. However, they must diligently avoid sectarian aggressiveness, local chauvinism and petty regionalism.

Comparisons

Comparison of events and personalities is a dangerous exercise for a historian as no two individuals or events are alike.

Style

The style of writing history is perhaps as important as the collection and analysis of material. History is a delightful creation, it is not just a mere post-mortem of facts. The style of presentation of the historical material, therefore, should have as much lucidity and flow as possible.

History is synonymous with change. It implies synthesis. It is interpretative. There is no doubt that history should be written and rewritten from time to time. As our outlook and concepts change, so our historical writings have to be revised.

Twelve

TRANSITION FROM THE ANCIENT TO THE MEDIEVAL PERIOD

VIJAY KUMAR THAKUR

PERIODISATION OF Indian history is a widely debated topic. At first the British historians divided Indian history into ancient, medieval and modern periods, but later it became fashionable with some text-books to term them Hindu, Muslim and British, on the basis of the people who dominated the political scene in the respective periods.

C.V. Vaidya marks three phases in the early history of India : Aryan (c. 4000 or 2000 B.C.—300 B.C.), Aryo-Buddhist or Buddhist (c. 300 B.C.-A.D. 600) and Hindu (c. A.D. 600-1200 or 1300)[1]. A similar line is taken by V.A. Smith who divides the early history of India into three sub-periods. Ancient India (from the earliest times to c. 322 B.C.), Hindu India (c. 322 B.C.—A.D. 647) and medieval Hindu Kingdoms or the Hindu period (c. A.D. 647—1200 or 1300)[2]. This scheme of periodisation smacks of communalism. Equally misleading is the periodisation attempted by official party-line Marxists who try to fit Indian history in the Marxian scheme of periods[3]. An open-minded Marxist historian concedes that "India showed a series of parallel forms which cannot be put into precise categories, for the mode based on slavery is absent, feudalism greatly different from the European type with serfdom and the manorial economy".[4] Thus, the whole problem has to be tackled afresh.

The period of transition from the ancient to medieval times is not easy to fix. The prevalent dates regarding the beginnings of medievalism in India reflect a pre-occupation with political developments which, in no way, reflect total history[5]. Periods in history do not begin and end on a particular day or year since fundamental changes in society occur over a long span of time. It is, moreover, not the beginning of decline or prosperity but the nature and degree of change in the existing society which determines the characteristics of a period[6]. The present system of dating ignores these points. It is the intervening phase during which distinctive factors mature to make their impact felt on society which divides the ancient from the medieval.

From the time of the Guptas one notices certain trends and features of feudalism which become widespread by the beginning of the 8th century A.D. The origins of this new formation have been sought in the land grants made to the brahmanas from as early as the 1st century A.D. From the middle of the 4th century A.D. such grants become frequent. Their two significant features are the transfer of all sources of revenue and the surrender of the police and administrative powers to the donees[7]. This led to the growth of powerful intermediaries in land who had considerable economic and political power. This new development can best be characterised as feudalism, the beginnings of which may be sought in the age of the Guptas and Harsha. This marks a period of transition in the history of India.

Because of the emerging feudal formation one discerns certain changes of vital importance from c. A.D. 700 onwards, which seem to herald the advent of a new age. The large scale transfers of land revenues and land to both secular and religious elements by princes and their vassals fostered a closed economy and led to commercial decline which is attested by the paucity of coins and the decline of urban centres in this period[8]. The policy of deliberate colonization through land grants was instrumental in the absorption of tribal and backward peoples and of their beliefs into the Brahmanical fold resulting in major changes in the religious sphere. This gave birth to an altogether new religion, Tantrism. Frequent land grants and partition of land led to the rise and growth of the Kayasthas[9]. The appearance of Rajputs on the Indian scene is another major development of this period. The most spectacular phenomenon was the proliferation of castes and religious sects which was a direct outcome of the strong sense of regionalism, fostered by the closed economy of this period. This sense of localism further gave birth to altogether new regional schools of art and architecture as well as to vernacular scripts and languages. The Sanskrit literature of this period lost its originality. The doctrines of *bhakti* and *karma* dominated the entire scene as they suited the feudal ideology.[10] They bred the spirit of unflinching loyalty and fatalism. The moral decline in this period, evident from the sculptures of Khajuraho and Konarak and the preponderance of sexual literature, led to certain basic changes in general outlook. The position of women deteriorated. The number of mixed castes as well as the untouchables increased and the pressure on land became acute. Even temporal morality declined and superstitions came to play an important role in society. Decentralisation in the political field became the norm of the day. The importance of agriculture further increased and that of industries declined. The introduction of Islam in Indian society brought about further changes[11].

It becomes obvious that the major changes in administrative, political, social and economic fields which led to the growth of a new system of life, took place during the 6th and 7th centuries A.D. The medieval period in Indian history, therefore, may be taken to begin from c. A.D. 700 as by this time the feudal institutions and feudal way of life had definitely unleashed a number of changes varying in nature and all pervasive in scope.

References

1. *History of Medieval Hindu India*, Vol. I (1921), Preface, p. 1.
2. cf. *Early History of India* (1924).
3. S.A. Dange, *India from Primitive Communism to Slavery* (1949).
4. D.D. Kosambi, *An Introduction to the Study of Indian History* (1956), p. 15.
5. For different views see V.K. Thakur, 'Periodisation of Indian History: The Transition From Ancient to Medieval Times',

L.N. Mishra Commemoration Volume, (to be published by the Bihar Research Society).

6. cf. R.S. Sharma, *Light on Early Indian Society and Economy(1966), p. 146.*
7. V.K. Thakur, 'Economic Changes in Early Medieval India (*c.* A.D. 600-1200)', *D.D. Kosambi Commemoration Volume,* (Ed. L. Gopal), (1977), p. 187.
8. *Ibid., passim.*
9. V.K. Thakur, 'Origin of the Kayasthas: A Historical Probing', *Journal of Historical Research,* Vol. XIX, No. 2, pp. 28-43.

10 See above p. 69-Ed.

11. For details of these developments see Idem, *L.N. Mishra Commemoration Volume.*

APPROACHES TO INDIAN HISTORY

Thirteen

CAN THERE BE OBJECTIVITY IN HISTORY

ASHOK VOHRA

LET US begin with an explanation of the word History. *The Oxford English Dictionary* describes 'history' as the continuous methodical record of public events; whole train of events connected with nations, persons, and things; aggregate of past events, course of human affairs. No historian will take this description very seriously. For it ignores (*a*) the obvious fact that all men and all events are not equally worth studying and that certain persons and certain achievements have value and significance which make them particularly deserving of our attention. Any historical narrative, therefore, besides being concerned with past human actions of specifiable kinds has also to limit itself to what is important or significant within the range, (*b*) that history is not merely a description of events like the beginning and the end of wars, beginning and end of revolutions and counter revolutions, reformation of religious institutions, conquests, depressions, careers or empires, parliaments and classes etc., it also attempts to explain why the event happened. A historian is, therefore, concerned with the question : why human beings in their own estimation acted as they did. It is in this activity that history distinguishes itself from stamp-collecting or antiquarianism etc. The intimate relation between facts, interpretation, and history can be summed up as : facts without their interpretative explanation are dead, and history without its facts is like a fairy tale.

My purpose in this paper is to show that history *cannot* logically be objective in the sense the natural sciences are. The central feature of objectivity in the natural sciences is that the conclusions, in their case, do not depend upon the value judgements of the investigator. Therefore, when I say that history cannot be objective, I mean that the conclusion that the historian arrives at cannot be independent of his value judgement. We shall see that both the facts with which the historian deals, and the explanations that he gives are subjective.

Let us begin with facts, the basic ingredient of history. The facts with which a historian is concerned are in the final analysis those about the relation of individuals to one another in society, and about the social forces released by the actions of individuals. The human actions that the historian takes into account can be divided into two types, *one* : the action of a person in his individual capacity, *two* : the action of a person in a group. Psychologists tell us that the two types of actions are radically different from one another. The subjective choice of the historian, therefore, enters in two ways at this stage. *First*, he may prefer the one type of action over the other as his subject of study. This choice necessarily depends upon his own commitments, purposes, motives and intentions. *Second*, not all human actions in society are of interest to a historian. He has to select out of the innumerable human actions a handful which he considers to be relevant and of significance for his purpose.

At this point subjectivity finds its entry in two ways. *One* : the facts are in themselves value-charged for they are human acts and human beings act with a purpose. They have motives and intentions; they make plans and their actions are in part determined by some goal they seek to achieve in future. *Two* : In the selection of the facts, the historian is necessarily guided by the values that he is committed to, or he cherishes. It is necessary because human nature being what it is, it is psychologically impossible to eliminate bias or prejudice from human selection. The criteria, therefore, that the historian lays down for the significance of any event is a subjective criteria. The search for an absolute or ideal principle of judgement which is divorced from society, or from the individual is a mirage.

I shall now consider the explanatory aspect of history. Any explanation of an event is at least the answer to either 'why it happened?' or to 'how it happened?' The first is called the causal approach, the latter, the functional approach. The question about 'how' can in principle be reduced to questions about 'why'. For, any explanation of how an event happened appeals to the 'logic of the situation' or to 'the inner logic of events'. This inevitably leads us to the question 'how that event came to be', and therefore, leads us back to the question 'why'.

To explain why an event had occurred is to state the cause/causes that brought it about. A historical event as we have said earlier is a result of, or culmination of, not one but several causes : physical, psychological, biological, sociological, technological, chance etc. The explanation that would be offered by any historian would highlight the cause which he prefers over the others. The preference would depend upon his interests, his commitments, his value judgements and his beliefs. Causal explanation in history is, therefore, bound up with interpretation and that, in turn, with the value-judgement of the historian. Moreover, the provisional selection of facts implies only a 'sketchy' explanation of an event or a process. The corelation of facts has to be provided by the historian. When doing so he enters the area of interpretation wherein his own purposes, and motives found expression.

Finally, all history whether descriptive or explanatory has to be in the ordinary language concepts. These are far from being neutral. Ordinary language provides us with a host of words, which describe the same state of affairs. The fact that the historian uses one set rather than another reflects his commitment to the values implied by it. This can be illustrated by taking an example of the various words that can be used for a discord between two parties, nations or groups. They are: feud, discord, conflict, strife, variance, contention, dissension, archiac, fight, battle, war, skirmish. If we look into the dictionary we find that though each word refers to the same state of affairs, the use of each word reflects our attitude towards the state of affairs.

The foregoing discussion shows that value judgements enter into history not accidentally or casually, but structurally and functionally. If I am right in holding this then it follows that all history is bound to reflect the value judgements of the writer, and is subjective.

Fourteen

NOTES ON APPROACHES TO INDIAN HISTORY

DEVAHUTI

The Necessity for Using Various Models

THERE IS disagreement about the use of models—the functional, and the dialectical for the interpretation of Indian history. The former perceives persistence and continuity, and works on the assumption that adjustment and convergence are ubiquitous in societies, the latter perceives traumatic breaks, and regards polarity and tension as ubiquitous in societies.

My first question is : is it imperative that only one single model be used? Is it, in fact, impossible to use both models, one at a time. Shouldn't one keep in mind the assumptions of each and examine historical material from both points of view?

Marx had made it his business to use one model for he had the mission to make history. The historian, by the rules of his game, should not make or make up history, either of the present or of the past and should not be fanatical about using only one interpretation, one framework.

Indian historians who do not use several models, in fact, work against themselves for their inclusive cultural tradition and plural present can never make efficient fanatics out of them. They suffer unnecessarily from a schizophrenia and a dilemma of definition of their approach to historiography.

I would adduce further support for it by the following observations. The intricacy and clarity at the same time, of the Indian mind comes through Indian literature. In the Panchatantra a story is boxed within a story and so on for a great length, and all these stories illustrate one common moral. It is almost as if the Indian game of chess were being rendered in the literary genre. In the Mahabharata, the main theme is interspersed with scores of other stories all forming an integral part of the larger maze-like yet harmonious pattern. Early Indian architecture embroidered with sculpture, often apparently, unconnected with it, or Indian music delighting in detours have the same characteristics.

The mind that thrives on this kind of creativity can never achieve consummation with the help of only one approach, however valid in its limited way. Its capacity is large, its horizon is wide, its sensitivity is deep. It has to have the challenge of variety with harmony.

My second question about the use of an exclusive model arises from the following comments. Marx's (1818-83) view of history was born from his response to *his* situation. Tension had become the dominant strand in the European situation and Marx was able to perceive it. But the earlier philosophers—social, political and religious, of the East and the West, also possessed perspicacity, awareness and vision.

Jaimini (500-200 B.C.), Kautilya (300 B.C. to A.D. 100), Samkara (788-820), Aurobindo (1872-1950), not to speak of a continual line of *prayaschita* writers from 12th to 18th centuries,[1] or Plato, Machiavelli, Kant, Hegel and Nietzsche had perceived the dominant strands in their own times, and had responded to them in their respective milieus—ancient, medieval or modern, Indian or European. Should we not see the past which was their present with their eyes rather than with ours. We would then know if the events and movements of those times respond today, largely to the functional or to the dialectical method.

Kautilya for example gave equal importance to the springs of consensus and conflict. He wrote : "*Anvikshiki* (*i.e.* Sankhya, Yoga and Lokayata, representing naturalist, metaphysical and materialist schools) is ever thought of as the lamp of all sciences, as the *means of all actions* and as *the support of all laws*". (1.2.12). (*italics ours*).

The point that I am trying to make—that terms and trends acquire new meaning with the passage of time, and that we should try to see the past in the idiom of the past (and certainly not for an axe to grind), was also dwelt upon in ancient times. The opening passage of the 3rd century A.D.-Sabarabhashya on Jaimini's Purva-mimamsa says :

> Loke yeshvartheshu prasiddhani padani tani sati sambhave tadarthanyeva sutrashviti avagantavyam. Nadhya haradibhih tesham parikalpaniyo-arthah paribhashitavyo va. Evam veda-vakyaneva ebhir-vyakhya-yante. Itaratha vedavakyani vyakhye-yani svapadarthascha vyakhyeyah iti prayatna gauravam syat.
>
> "The words of the Sutras are as far as possible, to be understood in that same sense which they are known to convey in common parlance; it is not right to assume for them, on the basis of elliptical and other devices, or to attribute to them, any special technical signification. It is the only way that all that would have to be done would be to explain the Vedic texts directly. Otherwise it would be necessary for us to explain the extraordinary and then the texts of the Veda. This would involve a great exertion" (Tr. Ganganatha Jha).

Discordance and Harmony : The Cynical Model

The dominant approach of the present times which I am trying to supplement with the multi-model approach, is the Marxian, because I think it takes a limited view of human nature and social reality. It views history in terms of discordance, it disregards the element of harmony. Zealous to the extent of being ruthless in its method it takes a cynical view of men and events and nourishes aggressive instincts at the expense of those energised by the force of love. It dulls the ability of adversaries to change places in their imagination in order to understand the other's state of mind.

Further it underplays the role of genetics as an inbuilt

cause of inequalities. To remove them and to reach the most idealist of ideals : from each according to his ability and to each according to his need, it does not advocate idealistic means *i.e.*, the transformation of the individual through morality although history bears witness to the effectiveness of morality for elevating human condition even if not totally and universally attained. The Marxian approach depends on external means pertaining to the System, which, however, can play a very strong supportive role.

Relationships between Society and State in Ancient and Medieval Times

The Communist argument leads to the birth of an immensely powerful state. The part played by it in Russia and China show it in practice. The lives of men are regulated through fear even if it be to avert hunger and inequality. The resultant tension sharpens class conflict. A deep unconscious hatred is generated in one class against the other for making it suffer the rule of fear and tension in order to achieve results. This further increases the power of the state.

While class interests clashed in ancient and medieval times their polarity could not have been so sharp, nor governed by fear, tension and hatred. The substitutes of these latter might have been disgust, indignation and righteous protest or perhaps patience, understanding and resignation. If the nature of the state and its methods of exercise of power were different over a period of millennia, the psyche of the clashing classes would have been different too, leading to an entirely different kind of relationship between state and society.

Models for measuring that relationship would have to be created by entering the ethos of those times. By going on reading till you hear the people speaking. For the essential matter of history is not what happened but what people felt about what happened. That is the reality of the times. It is of little consequence whether *we* think it was ugly, beautiful or indifferent.

Comparing and Contrasting the Marxian and the Traditional Indian Approaches to Change

Any Indian, with the Hindu cyclical view of life and the Buddhist explanation of phenomena through causation will consider the central feature of Marx's thought *i.e.*, an organic process of transformation and development, as a reflection of his own systems of thought.

But while Marx with his Semitic and Baptist psyche—linear, definitive, exclusive—has emphasised conflict as the moving force in transformation resulting in traumatic change, the autochthonous Indian thought has emphasised consensus (obviously arrived at through conflict) which because of the continuous correctives inherent in it does not think in terms of trauma or revolution as the moving force in transformation.

The difference in emphasis leads to life-views poles apart—one primarily cynical the other primarily idealist. One regarding the change of system as fundamental, the other regarding the change of heart in the individual as fundamental. Obviously one supports the other, either for good or for bad. The question is which is more basic and important of the two, the system or the individual.

If I may be permitted an aside here, it would be interesting to investigate in what way did the springs of Chinese autochthonous thought differ from the Indian to give birth to Mao in China and to Gandhi in India.

Distinction between Personal and Class Level Problems and Solutions

If the question be asked whether the same laws cause antagonisms at the personal level as at the class level and are the same solutions applicable for resolving them at both levels, the answer, I think, would be negative. Many social and economic problems, specially in agrarian societies, have to be dealt with at the personal level. The ruthlessness and apparent self-sufficiency that can be exercised between individuals and groups in industrial, highly monetized societies with institutionalised living, with hospitals, banks, courts, entertainments, educational centres etc., cannot be indulged in at the personal level between human beings.

The system—and the class-view of individuals assumes greater importance in industrialised societies and in urban areas, whereas the individual, even as a member of a large family, assumes greater importance in agrarian societies and in rural areas. India in the past was even more agrarian and rural than she is today—and with her own set of attitudes and values. Can the historian then justifiably apply models appropriate for 19th century Europe when trying to reconstruct ancient Indian society? This, of course, does not mean that he can make medieval Europe his frame of reference for understanding ancient or medieval India.

The Importance of the Ideal. The Chasm between extremes need not be viewed as hypocrisy.

The gap between the extremes of *dharma* and *artha,* or of *dharma* and *kama* has sometimes been described as the area of hypocrisy, thus, on the one hand, the ideal of *aparigraha*—non-possession, and on the other, a passionate plea for the pursuit of wealth; the ideal of *brahmacharya*, and the uninhibited expression of sensuousness through sculpture and literature. But the view may have been taken that the highest denominator, or the one most difficult to achieve should be made the point of reference. For the same reason *artha* was advised to be pursued in accordance with *dharma*, and *kama* was abstracted into the love divine.

Had the basic necessities of *artha* and *kama* not been tempered by the ideal with an opposite pull, society would have gone headlong in the initial direction until necessities would have become exaggerated into baneful luxuries. On the other hand, had *dharma* not been tempered by including *artha*, and *kama* in the *trivarga* system it might have become an aberration.

Tension is essential for balance. The weakness of a materialist philosophy would lie in not providing it through emphasis on *dharma* and *kama*, and of a renunciatory philosophy in not providing it through *artha* and *kama*.

The Necessity for Using Various Models Reiterated, — Art

If religion is the opium of the masses so is art, and man cannot live without either. The historian would therefore do well to take note of both.

Of the three operations that the historian performs—observation, reasoning and reporting, he should particularly take the literary writers' help in the first—he should allow their perception to sharpen his moral senses so that he can see the multitude of motives and inspirations behind every act. Scientific reasoning and reporting would follow automatically.

Exact perception of that which is individualistic, and response to 'here and now' leads to universality in writers of the literary genre. They may not point it out as such, the reader recognises it for himself. The larger the number of those who recognise it and the longer the period of time over which they do so the greater the measure of the universality. In the same way the exactly-perceived-case-studies of the scientific historian help arrive at generalisations proved by the test of time and space. They serve as laws to the extent that human responses do to given stimuli in given circumstances. This is not to overlook the fact that there is no exact repetition of situations.

"Art and Science offer very different neighbor models for the study of social science, and would prompt different selections of its qualities-to-be-explained, and different explanations of its successes and shortcomings." (Stretton, H., *The Political Sciences 1972,* p. 421). One may, for example, compare Jane Austen's and David Riesman's judgements of social conformity. Through such comparisons the immediate purposes and methods of social science as well as its social effects would be recognised to be different. The means or models would have thus affected the end or conclusions. Nothing can emphasise more the need for various models for the historian, both to understand the past and through its interpretation to create a present that will shape the future.

The Problem of Identification

Universal and Unique

It is true that the raw data for the study of societies, such as specific values, institutions, customs and cultural forms are not the same as their conceptional abstractions which constitute the basis of sociological categories. However, it is not right that those who ask for an Indian view of history or of sociology be dismissed as suffering from the ideology of nationalism.

Conceptual abstractions are not arrived at in a vacuum and one's basic assumptions do affect ones understanding of the raw data which is to be reduced to conceptual abstractions for creating a frame of reference. The basic level having been crossed, complexities which can only be termed as uniquenesses, appear. For example an Indian may question a very basic-level-abstraction—the English term religion—which he will find much too narrow for his purposes. He will, almost certainly, also question the 'great tradition', 'little tradition' categories for the over-preciseness and value judgement they entail.

A universalitic frame-work, therefore, does not always serve the purpose, nor does it serve the whole purpose. There is a case for an Indian frame of reference specially at this stage in our evaluation of history when it suffers from handicaps both in the matter of tools and methodology. For example, the language of the sources is not sufficiently known-much less mastered, ancient terms have not been understood in their proper sense, and existing methods of approach have not been taken cognizance of, much less any new ones independently worked out.

References

1. e.g. Bhava-deva-bhatta (12th), Sulapani (14th-15th), Rudra-dhara (15th), Vachaspati (15th), Govind-ananda (16th), Raghu-nandana (16th), Todar-ananda (16th), Nanda-pandita (16th-17th), Mitra-misra (17th), Nila-kantha (17th), Nagoji-bhatta (18th).

Fifteen

THE REDUNDANCIES AND THE LACUNAE IN INDIAN HISTORIOGRAPHY

B.P. SINHA

THE HISTORIAN of ancient India is handicapped by the nature and quantum of his sources. Biographies, laudatory inscriptions, dharma-sutras, and dharma-sastras are valuable in reconstructing and reinterpreting history and giving a feel for the civilization of India, but they are inadequate for attempting a critical assessment of the past. The paucity of material prevents him from being able to look at the other side of the medal. For instance Samudragupta's Allahabad prasasti does not have any supportive evidence from the south regarding his campaigns in that part of the country. Nor has Sasanka a biography like Harsha. The ancient historian perforce uses 'likely', 'may be', 'perhaps' etc., much more often than he would like to.

When the West first discovered 'ancient India' for the world including India, they were enthralled by its literary excellence for the period it belonged to, and by its great monuments of art and architecture. The philosophies of India, particularly of the Upanishads and Buddhism swept them off their feet, probably because of lack of such visions in contemporary Western philosophy. Naturally they appeared to give low priority to ancient Indian material civilisation, quest for wealth and even to its political structures and administrative apparatuses. To impute ulterior motives to nineteenth century Western savants for this, to me, is not just. It would be as naive to condemn them for their lack of appreciation of our ancient political institutions or quest for material things as to condemn the modern West for not getting impressed by our technological and industrial development. It is true that Vincent Smith led the group of Western scholars, who emphasised the running theme of centrifugal forces in the political field in India before the advent of the British Raj. This may have served the purpose of justifying the Raj to a resurgent India. But can we deny the fact that politically India had been more divided than united in her long history. No one can completely overcome the predilections of the time, and the westerners including the British were no exception. This so-called imperialist approach to Indian History should be examined in the context of the rival approach of militant nationalism. K.P. Jayaswal's Hindu Polity is a good example of an overstatement as a rejoinder to Western ignorance or negligence, may be wilful, of Indian achievements in this particular field. Both the imperialist and nationalist approaches to the writing of Indian history suffer from the failing not only of seeing only one side of the medal but also of gloating over it uncritically.

The Marxist approach too is both unscientific and unhistorical. Marx certainly did great a service to the understanding of history by emphasising the part played by economic factors. He thereby showed the inadequacy of understanding a people and their history on the basis of religion, philosophy, literature or political system to the exclusion of their economic system. It is true that one does not live by bread alone but it is truer that one cannot live without bread. The material life of the common people, their economic and technological progress, the class controlling the economic power—all these factors certainly mould a country's history and culture. But the Marxist mistake lies in overdoing this. The place of the individual in history - of a Napolean, a Buddha or, an Asoka cannot be underestimated. Today even some Marxists concede that 'heroes' are important in the crucial moments of Historical Divides. The Marxist approach emphasising the materialist aspects of civilization has led them to glorify the Kushana age and underplay the Gupta age mainly on the basis of the discoveries of relatively poor architecture in the Gupta strata compared to the Kushana strata. Against this it may be pointed out that some monuments of the Gupta period like the Devgarh temple, the Aphsad temple and others do not prove architectural decay. Anyhow the crucial point is that over-emphasis on material excellence or decay does not do proper justice to any civilization at any point of time. Culture is not only agriculture and architecture. The literary, educational, religious and philosophical outpourings of the Gupta Age freed from the trammels of foreign strings place it on a much higher pedestal than the Kushana. The obsession with one type of source led Woolly, absolutely wrongly, to characterise Vedic civilisation as barbaric. The Marxist approach is basically inadequate, and often mischievous in seeing one to the exclusion of the many truths of history.

The only scientific approach to Indian historiography is to note the facts as known, and to weave them into a story, weak or strong, depending on whether the facts are full or partial. As there are still enormous gaps in his sources, the historian may have to withhold his conclusions many times. Often, much against his will, he may also have to give more prominence to one or the other aspect of history and culture depending on the nature and quantum of sources available to him at the time. For instance a historian of the Vedic period normally devotes more space to religion and philosophy than to political history, art and economic history. But he need not, rather, should not, give the impression that these aspects did not matter to the Vedic Aryans. He must admit at the outset that the sources being partial, a fuller picture may await future discoveries. A historian should try, as best as possible, to follow the ideal set by Kalhana—to act as a judge, who tries to examine the case on the basis of the evidence before him. Aware of his built-in biases and prejudices, he must try to overcome them while collecting and evaluating the evidence pertaining to his subject.

A historian of India, moreover, should take an integrated

view of the history of the entire sub-continent. Only if he would devote as much attention to the northern as to the southern part of the country would he be able to give a logical and well-reasoned account of events as they took place or of schools and movements as they arose, developed and culminated.

For this reason, deep and extensive regional histories would be welcome. The emphasis, moreover, should not be on political events but on the cultural components of history. Finally the historian should address himself as much to the phenomena of change as to those of stability.

Sixteen

THE USES AND AIMS OF HISTORY

B.N. PURI

THE STUDY of history is sometimes dubbed as metaphysical nonsense for it has no lesson to teach us and the conclusions from its lessons, if any, need not be true for all times. There may be some golden grains on the sand of time, but the past is always wiped out. It goes down into the pit and then everything starts afresh. History whether past or present is supposed to be just a magic show with little rhyme or reason, and with no lesson for us which might guide our future path.

As against this concept there is a more widely accepted one that history has a part to play in our national life. It is a discipline that makes sense of the past in relation to the present, and conversely, of the present in the context of the past. The lessons of history stand not to distract us but to inspire us. History has a practical value like the experience of wise parents. In the words of Ranke, 'History must be an interpretation of the past in order to serve as a guide for the future'. Consciousness of the past does not impose any brake on action in the present, rather it heightens resolve, sharpens perception and quickens reaction. The lessons of history, however, have to be conveyed through a skilled historian, mature, experienced and balanced in thought. He cannot tailor history to a pattern or subject it to a formula or a master concept. The historian must correlate the social, the economic, and the political forces which are kept in separate compartments by the specialists.

According to Sir Keith Hancock, there are three cardinal virtues which distinguish the great historian from the crowd of journeymen, namely attachment, justice and span. Attachment is the very opposite of detachment. Not impartiality or objectivity are the historian's initial task, but getting close to people, getting inside situations should be his objective. The chameleon-like faculty of the historian sets up a tension from which is born the virtue of justice or fairness to redress the balance between different attachments. Justice is the cure for the perversion of attachments. The third virtue span is the awareness of the background. It places the object of immediate or intense study in its proper perspective with other objects, near or distant, to which it is related.

These three principles, applied to historical writings might as well be called historical imagination, historical architecture, and historical reflection, presupposing historical criticism, technique of scholarship, and mastery of sources. By historical imagination is meant the deep inclination towards the past, the desire to enter the past, to understand it and re-enact it. Historical imagination is necessary for the historian. The problem of historiography is well described as the resurrection of life in its entirety. Historical imagination and historical architecture or span put the object of study in proper perspective while historical reflection demands correct interpretation of historical forces working in different situations.

The study of history should be of real use in practical, specially in political life. It need not be only a form of poetry recording the more dramatic acts of kings, warriors and statesmen free from the encumberances of metrical rules. It should portray human character, breathing nobler sentiments and stimulating pious actions. It should serve as a guide to consecrate the noble past and furnish a key for the future. In the words of Churchill, "Pondering over the past may give guidance in days to come, enabling a new generation to repair some of the damages of the past years, and thus govern in accordance with the needs and glory of man''. History and historical study should serve as a compass for political guidance. There is no better safeguard than the study of history to guard against the corrupting influence of power. In this task of writing history it is equally necessary not to paint a picture with the choicest colour thereby displaying one's interest or partiality for any hero or situation. The successive phases of national well-being, the rise, fall and change of political situations, the dominant ideas prevailing in different periods should form the subject of study for the historian. He should try to deduce lessons about the conditions on which the well being of the society depends. In other words, the study of history should include not only political situations but also the socio-economic, cultural and religious tensions all taken as different, equally important, facets of one composite whole. The past is a store house of knowledge and fund of experience. Its material is indispensable to man and can serve as a corrective to his wrong notions.

Another approach to the study of history, as suggested by Toynbee, could be to strike a balance between our allegiance to our country and its history and displaying a wider outlook according to which the human race coalesces into a single society; in other words, looking at history in universal terms. Sudden confrontations of peoples, civilizations and religions, that had previously been strangers to each other, might have resulted in the destruction and uprooting of the weaker of them and their cultural traditions, but in return they gave a new vitality—a change in the quality of civilisation they invaded and into which their descendants got assimilated. This movement and cross fertilisation is common to all cultures. Thus, history has to be looked at in universal terms with the perspective that the goal of human social endeavour is the unification of the human race, thereby eliminating the tension between the universal common humanity and the pigment local differences in superficial manners and customs. It is one of the paradoxes of the present age that the prevalent schools of historians work under the spell of parochial nationalism, or conform to a dogmatic ideological approach. Both should be avoided as disruptive forces in the modern world. Science and technology tend towards unification, and the need is great to second them through the conscious and deliberate work done by modern historians. The history of mankind is the sum total of all human efforts. Human history has to be seen as a unity.

In the light of the above observations, the study of our country's history has to be undertaken in proper perspective without reservation or commitment, but not ignoring the geographical factor in Indian history. Further, no historian can afford to ignore the great spiritual heritage built up over a long period of time. This fact has to be appreciated and fitted into the texture of history which records the march of events and the political transformations in the country. Nowhere else has there been such a synthesis of different religious and cultural ideas as in our country. That is the rhythm to which the historical events have to be matched.

It is, therefore, absolutely necessary that the history of our country be viewed not from any one particular angle. It should concentrate on recording facts in a truthful manner and in proper perspective. Here one is reminded of Niebuhr, who pointed out, "In laying down the pen we must be able to say in the sight of God", 'I have not knowingly, nor without earnest investigation written anything which is not true'. The study of history is now fast deviating from the great ideal of truth in the name of patriotism, communal harmony, national integration, secularism and all such high-sounding phrases and jargon. One cannot deviate from truth for any consideration. Ranke, also pointed out, "I found by comparison that the truth was more interesting and beautiful than romance. I turned away from it and resolved to avoid all invention and imagination in my works and stick to fact."

The present gathering of historians interested in projecting the true history and culture of the country must keep in view several points. Firstly, we cannot cut Indian history into bits calling them ancient medieval or modern, or Hindu, Muslim and British. In fact, we must all stress on the unity of history and that too of the country as a whole. Secondly, local pigments of culture must also form part of the study.

There has to be a broad spectrum for the academic historian who should be free from bias or prejudice. He is not expected to distort facts to suit his thesis. He should study the source material exhaustively before coming to any conclusions. Here one may quote the views of Sir Jadunath Sarkar : "I would not care whether truth is pleasant or unpleasant and in consonance with or opposed to current views. I would not mind in the least whether truth is or is not a blow to the glory of my country. If necessary, I shall bear in patience the ridicule and slander of friends and society for the sake of preaching the truth, understand truth, and accept truth. This should be the firm resolve of a historian".

Seventeen

PAST PREJUDICES AND PRESENT CHALLENGES

D. AWASTHI

CLIO, THE Muse of History, deserves to be better served than we in India have so far done. The only approach to our country's history that was recognised or encouraged by the foreign rulers was the one that suited their interests; and this was doubtlessly vitiated by the usual racial and imperialist bias that characterizes the average European when he looks at Oriental history and civilization. Even the more distinguished among them could not rise above the besetting vice of prejudice. They worked within a limited framework—they counted their trophies and gloated over the defeat of others. Most Indian scholars who were nurtured in the school of history, which, for want of a better nomenclature, may be called 'Anglo-Indian', echoed consciously, or at times un-consciously, what their foreign counterparts were fond of repeating; and thus they proved more passionate than even their masters in their praise of all that the British did, and in condemnation of whatever the Indians rendered. Under these circumstances, a really objective history of India could not have been attempted successfully.

Here I am restricting myself to the British period of Indian history only. The old approach to the British period was misleading and biased. The European scholars with the notion that British rule in India was a blessing for the country and that it was the British who had rescued

India from age-old anarchy and confusion, dwelt at length on the faults and foibles of the Indian people and acted as advocates of British rule rather than as impartial judges of events. They were also obsessed with the view that the English records alone could reveal the whole truth, and so they had little inclination to discover or utilize the evidence on the Indian side such as that on the Marathas or the Sikhs. They looked upon the annexations of a Wellesley or a Dalhousie as acts of dynamic statesmanship, while they dubbed those of an Akbar as instances of cupidity and lust for conquest, or of a Shivaji as the working of a 'mountain rat'. In their eyes, the Europeans could do no wrong, or did so only under exceptional and fully extenuating circumstances.

It is now upto Indian historians to place together from all kinds of data a true and objective history of the Indian people, and check the old notions on the basis of raw materials of history hitherto imperfectly known or even kept away from the reach of the historian. It is, however, necessary to remember that the reaction against the old approaches should not lead us to the extremes of chauvinism, sectarianism, communalism, casteism, or provincialism. There should not also be any political twist to history. The danger is not unreal, for already there are symptoms of an unhealthy zeal to idolize the past and defend everything that is indigenous. Such ultrapatriotic school of Indian history will not lead to a correct reconstruction of our national history and, in the long run, may prove to be as unsound and unhistorical as the old Anglo-Indian school. However unpalatable, the Indian historian must not shrink from stating the truth.

The Indian historian must also beware of the various pitfalls in his path today. There is the danger that he may develop a communal outlook, and may see everything from the Hindu or Muslim point of view. Regional and provincial feelings may also sway the outlook of the historian, and he may be tempted to present the history from his own local angle, or he may choose to align himself with a particular caste or social group, and give a wrong turn to the presentation of his subject. Lastly, our historian runs the risk of being influenced by party prejudices or political loyalties. If he makes himself the apologist for any particular party, he will cease to be an impartial narrator and will degenerate into a mercenary publicity officer.

Another conspicuous factor about Indian History writing is that hitherto it has been the history of kings and wars of particular dynasties and regions, of the administration of Viceroys and of their family connexions, of the recital of the lists of the Secretaries of State, the transfers and promotions of petty district officials and the like ; but not that of the people and their life, society, art and culture. The historian of today and tomorrow will have to concern himself more with social, economic and cultural aspects than with wars and invasions and royal dynasties. Political events cannot of course be ignored, for they form the fabric of history. But this is no time to believe with Carlyle in the decisive importance of 'heroes'. In our opinion, biographies of ordinary men ought to be written.

The historian will have to make an inductive as well as an objective approach to his subject. He will have to produce a more intrinsic and correlated picture of the life of the common man. Institutions, cultural or otherwise, will have to be studied not in isolation, as hitherto done but in relation to each other. The interrelation of history with other social sciences will also have to be borne in mind. This work will have to be achieved by us in planned stages and by cooperative effort since the process of rewriting Indian history calls for an enterprise which is beyond the powers of any single man or group or even a generation.

Eighteen

SERVICE AND DISSERVICE TO HISTORY

AJAY MITRA SHASTRI

HISTORY IS the outcome of man's craving to know his past. He has been as eager to know about his past as about future, and this twofold curiosity has given rise to history and astrology. From a common man's viewpoint the historian would have served him well if he gave him a reasonably authentic account of his early surroundings and various stages of development to the present times. But the historian, could not remain unaffected by various contemporary pressures. History writing suffered in the process and history became a tool for serving ulterior motives.

A study of modern Indian historiography well illustrates this point. The British historians who initiated the study of Indian history in modern times were often members of the administrative services. They served their own cause by seeking to prove that conditions in pre-British period were anarchical, law and order having been established by the British for the first time. When the Indians launched a struggle for emancipation they too, discerned vast possibilities in historical writing to serve their own cause. For them all that was great happened in India's past. At the same time we also had our share of communalist historical writing as well as of one sect against the other within the same religious system. Religion which through various revivalist movements had served a constructive purpose by heightening national consciousness was, in fact, one of the causes for this kind of writing. Of the political ideologies that affected the writing of history Marxism has exercised the strongest influence. According to it all historical events are to be interpreted in terms of economic processes with the object of proving Marx's theory that all human relationships are dependent primarily on the control over the means of production. Histories with a racial bias were written too, suggesting the superiority of one race over another, *e.g.*, Aryans over Dravidians or vice versa. These have, in turn, been generally taken to indicate the superiority of one region, north or south, over the other. Even within the region the rulers of a given area were given extra importance because the historians responsible happened to belong to it. Sometimes one comes across the extraordinary phenomenon of such historians lamenting the absence of an annalist or biographer for their chosen hero and their consequent inability to project him in a better light than his rival. One may further mention some recent efforts to write history on caste lines with the deliberate aim of proving the superiority of their favourite, often their own, caste.

We thus see several strains in modern Indian historical writing. In this varied exercise history as such has often lost its own identity. It has become subservient to certain objectives. As it is treated as just a means to serve a particular, generally narrow, objective, known facts are ignored or suppressed or given an unwarranted meaning. Certain factors are deliberately given undue importance at the cost of other equally important factors. As a result of these strains, historical writing has become narrow, one-sided and distorted.

Whatever be the merits or demerits of specific ideologies or isms, and many of them have served some useful purpose at one time or another, should we as historians lose our own identity as historians and become mere propagators of ideologies distorting our historical vision and that of our readers?

The primary duty of a historian, I think, is to be faithful

to his profession. Of course, being a social creature he is not, and cannot be expected to be isolated and totally uninfluenced by his surroundings. But it is his responsibility to ensure that his personal faith and ideology do not distort his vision and interfere with his historical writing. Otherwise he does great disservice to the cause of his chosen discipline as well as to his readers.

[illegible] discussion [illegible] balance between [illegible] creative [illegible] and [illegible] by [illegible] unimpressed by his [illegible] rich and [illegible] his [illegible] Otherwise he does [illegible] nor the cause of his [illegible] as well as [illegible]

Nineteen

HISTORICAL DISTORTIONS - THEIR REASONS AND REMEDY

A.R.G. TIWARI

ONE OF our most urgent tasks after independence was to rewrite Indian history from the national point of view to bring out both the strength and the weakness of our social, economic, religious, cultural and political institutions which may, on the one hand, account for the loss of our political freedom and, on the other hand, explain our ultimate success in regaining freedom from the conquerors. But our historians failed us miserably. They were not able to evolve an original assessment of their history nor able to discard foreign models. This failure should be regarded as one of the greatest cultural tragedies comparable in its magnitude to the defeat of our armies at Panipat and Plassey. Nor is the present scene very hopeful. Our guidelines and frame-work are still those which were laid down by foreign historians in the colonial era. The antipathy of that school of historians towards some of our most valuable sources of information not only continues but is intensified in several instances. Our present day historians lack a sense of direction. One can, therefore, legitimately ask : Are we culturally and spiritually free?

There were some understandable reasons for the appearance of distorted history books during British rule. Many of the historians of that period were either British administrators or official historians. Their works were full of obvious or subtle bias. It should be admitted that some British and many non-British foreign Indologists of this period were persons of great integrity, scholarship and detachment. Many of them had great sympathy for India and great admiration for Indian classics and Indian philosophy. But even they were handicapped by their subconscious, social and cultural bias emanating from their orientation, intellectual and moral. They had no emotional rapport with our way of life. Therefore, they also misunderstood or faintly understood the historical role of our social ideals or social institutions.

In addition to these historians there were the uncharitable foreign Christian missionaries, many of whom, being more zealous than competent or honest, fabricated or exaggerated Indian social evils to justify their missionary activities among a people in need of redemption. These missions at times acted as a covert wing for British political activities. The Indian Christian scholars often enthusiastically followed the same line to console their uneasy conscience for giving up ancestral values of life along with the time-honoured religion of their forefathers. The Persian-knowing historians—both Hindu and Muslim—were also guilty of partisanship as they made no use of non-Persian native sources.

No less blameworthy were our 'patriotic' historians who went to the other extreme in their political prejudice and produced distorted and falsified accounts of our past. The objective of some was to strengthen national morale by glorifying the ancient past. Others, in order to achieve communal harmony, specially for the purpose of strengthening the national struggle for independence, ignored Muslim excesses or dramatised their ordinary acts of good governmet during the Sultanate and Mughal periods. Underplaying Hindu resistance to some Muslim policies during this time was a result of the same attitude. The periodization of our history contains the same fallacy. Muslim rulers did not rule over the whole country during the 'Muslim' period. What is more important is that the national culture was non-Muslim.

A fresh appraisal of our history should convey the

mutual interaction, inter-dependence and inter-penetration of the political, intellectual, spiritual, aesthetic, moral, social and economic forces. To achieve this we should examine both the current norms of historical research, and the norms of evaluation of our source material. Our present norms address themselves to the problems of English, European or American historiography. Some of the factors that will determine our historiography are the country's antiquity, diversity, the nature of source materials, and psychological handicaps as well as plus points. We should spare some time for a systematic study of the problem. Some centres like the history laboratory at the Sardar Patel University in Gujarat should be established in suitable institutions which, besides judging the validity, suitability and potential of current norms, should also develop fresh norms and guidelines. They should also prepare exhaustive lists of source materials. These should be available in clear-cut charts for the benefit of researchers. Without such ground work and fundamental research in historical methodology appropriate for the study of our civlisation our efforts can not bear fruit.

multidimensional interdependence and inter-penetration of the political, intellectual, spiritual, aesthetic, moral, social and economic forces. To achieve this we should examine both the current norms of historical research and the norms of evaluation of our source material. Our present points address themselves to the problems of English, European or American historiography. Some of the factors that will determine our historiography are the country's situation vis-a-vis the nature of source materials, and psychological handicaps as well as plus points. We should prepare some time for systematic study of the problem. Some centres like the history laboratory at the Sardar Patel University in Gujarat should be established in all state institutions which besides judging the validity, reliability and potential of current norms should also develop fresh norms and guidelines. They should also prepare exhaustive lists of source materials. These should be available in clear cut charts for the benefit of researchers. Without such ground work and fundamental research in historical methodology appropriate for the study of our civilisation our efforts can not bear fruit.

Twenty

PROBLEMS OF FRAMEWORK AND METHODOLOGY

RAGHAVENDRA VAJPEYI

Puranam ityeva na sadhu sarvam,
na capi kavyam navam ityavadyam;
Santah pariksyanyatarad bhajante,
mudhah parapratyaya neyabuddhih.

(EVERY THING old does not become desirable because it happens to be old; and the poetry does not, automatically, become worthy of deprecation because of its being new; after ascertaining the merit of a thing, knowledgeable people accept one or the other, only a blockhead is guided by others' views and not an intelligent person.)

This stanza from Kalidasa's Malavikagnimitra (Act I, verse 2) written about fifteen hundred years ago may inspire the historian to rewrite and to reinterpret history. The need to rewrite history is imperative because of the changes wrought, slowly but surely, in the thinking processes of each generation of historians. It is the accumulated and pervasive social consciousness as crystalised in his own time that reveals itself through the writings of the historian, ancient, medieval or modern.

The mature historian of today, for instance would find it wasteful to demolish either the imperialist or the nationalist interpretation of history; the need for it is no longer there. However, the historian is a social being who cannot remain unaffected by his environment. He would therefore feel the need to demolish or to build up a different set of theories when rewriting history.

Of one thing he may be sure. There is no single factor that affects change in the historical process and no overriding factor for all places and all times. Nothing has vitiated historical writing more than the erroneous belief that the opposite is true.

History is the sum total of ecology, knowledge of the technical know-how and the will to master it, as well as the response of society to various historical situations, *i.e.* social psychology. Individuals with original ideas who succeeded in conveying them to contemporary society also contributed to the shaping of history.

As regards the search for models and frameworks for different periods and sub-periods of Indian history their relevance for the study in question should be the main criterion. All models would have relative validity. Bias for or against any single one would militate against a scientific approach to history. Where indigenous models exist and offer better answers, clinging to alien ones would be nothing short of a pedantic approach to Indian history.

For attempting a reconstruction of Indian history in general, and of the ancient period in particular, the following might serve as our terms of reference :

1. The growth of state power and awareness of class interests affected change in the basic relationship between economy and social psychology; dependence of the latter on the former, was reversed.

2. The social and political *elite* in Indian history had, on many occasions, entered into compromises in order to protect their respective class interests. Their hand-in-glove policies were responsible for deterioration of a progressive social psychology into a static one and, later on, into that of retrogression.

3. The classical Gupta society which was responsible for unprecedented progress in various fields of human activity, such as science and technology, literature and the fine arts, failed to make its gains permanent. Its rulers, in spite of the twin qualities of dynamic leadership and capacity to face a variety of challenges, failed to realise the

importance of economic realities. They did not try out the agrarian system which had shown remarkable results during the Mauryan age.

4. More often than not the social and political *elite* pursued short term policies which adversely affected the progress of society.

5. The importance of individual consciousness, apart from group consciousness in affecting change in historical processes, should be taken into account. The examples of two individuals may be cited. Kalidasa's progressive views on the position of women and sudras find their best expression in the *Abhijnana Sakuntala*. The same work, in the dialogue between the fisherman and the police, records the author's protest against the oppression of the weak. Later the king is made aware of the weaknesses of the system (Act V vv.21-30; Act VI v.iff; Act I vv. 1-2. Also see *Malavikagnimitra* Act I vv. 1-2). Though an idealist and a puritan, Kabir was a non-conformist. He criticised both Hindus and Muslims and was least concerned about the reactions of the orthodoxy.

importance of [illegible]. They did not try to [illegible] which [illegible] shown remarkable [illegible]

[illegible] more [illegible] than [illegible]

[illegible] should be taken into account. The examples of two [illegible] view of [illegible] of women and [illegible] in the [illegible] the dialogue between the [illegible] the authors [illegible] a [illegible] and illusions and [illegible] the [illegible] of the orthodoxy.

Twenty-One

THE IMPERATIVES OF HISTORIOGRAPHY-FREEDOM AND GLOBAL CONTEXT

L.B. KENNY

THE PURPOSE of all human endeavour, individual as well as collective, is attainment of freedom in an ever-increasing measure. This freedom is not only a rational and moral concept, inherent in every individual, but is also a progressive disappearance of all restrictions on the unfolding of the potentialities of individuals as human beings. Historical writing cannot develop unless there is a suitable climate of freedom for development. In fact, intellectual and academic freedom is a fundamental pre-requisite for historical writing. Any restriction on the historian's objective thinking and expression of free, frank and critical historical evaluation is dangerous to the progress of historical writing. It is indeed very unhealthy if a historian is penalised for expressing his independent opinion on a subject of history because his views are not in tune with the prevailing popular emotions and beliefs associated with the subject concerned. Gathering courage to disagree with the set views of conventional historians is one of the greatest challenges of Indian historical writing today.

An atmosphere free from fear, prejudice or malice is very vital for any history seminar. The 'scientific' spirit of enquiry is to be conveyed through the voice of reason and fair-play and not through biased political ideologies.

History is an old discipline. But unfortunately its worth

as a humanistic discipline is not understood in our country. Compared to the great studies in this field in the Western countries, we have little to show. There is, for instance, a stagnation in the study of Indian historiography in our country. Unless we strive to become a part of the international history discipline, any approach to the study and writing of Indian history would be meaningless. Unless our history is related to the contemporary developments in Asia, Africa and Europe, it may lose its full significance. Our approach should reflect what we are today; what we have been in the past is a part and parcel of all humanity. Even our national history, I feel, would gain added significance in a wider setting. Sectarian, or communal or national sentiment has no place in modern historical writing. One should never forget that ancient Indian history has its roots in many lands and among many peoples.

History being "a dialogue continually going on between the past and the present with an eye to the future" (Carr, *What is History*?), each age emerges with fresh questions to ask of the past, and inevitably offers fresh answers and assessments with a richer content than in the previous age. Much of our thinking, therefore, has to be broadened with new perspectives, fresh challenges and modern historical dimensions. History shall never have any meaning in a static society; a blind reverence for the past, therefore, would never take us forward.

Twenty Two

INSCRIPTIONS AND HISTORIOGRAPHY

K. V. SOUNDARA RAJAN

1. Case history

THE PAPER suggests an optimum utilisation of case histories found in inscriptions as a method for understanding the *ethos* of the concerned communities and leaders, at a given stage of history. We shall take up the following examples :—

(1) restoration of the original award of land, as mentioned in the Velvikudi Grant of Maranjadaiyan Pandyan *c.* A. D. 8th century.

(2) Arbitration of Appanna Dandanayaka in the Tirumayam record (*c.* A. D. 13th century) adjudicating between two adjacent temples of Sivaism and Vishnuism.

(3) Arbitration of Bukkaraya in the Sravanabelgola abhayasasana record (*c.* 14th century A. D.), between Jainas and Vishnuites there.

In the first instance, a recipient brings to the notice of the king the grant of land by his predecessor to him (or his ancestors) which had been taken away during the subsequent *inter regnum*, and wants the restoration of his right to that property. The king, after examining the situation, gives his extempore decision in the applicant's favour. The political and legal implications of this royal decision would be significant.

In the second case, a very detailed adjudication in all aspects of mutual bickerings was given by the military dictator who was acting on behalf of an aggressor Hoysala king when he had occupied Tamil Nadu. He discharged his functions in an exemplary manner, notwithstanding the political situation. He even went to the extent of declaring as null and void any earlier record in favour of one or the other of the contending parties, that might be found engraved on the body of the temples. In this over-enthusiasm in giving effect to this, he erased out of the rock-face a unique musical inscription of early 8th century A. D. as he could not get it deciphered satisfactorily. This incidentally, reflects on the state of academic interest among the intelligentsia in *their* past heritage. Anyhow they were more interested in their *current* rights, but these rights had to be examined by a process of arbitration, under the political agent.

In the third case, the award by the king puts the onus for damaging or destroying the religious places of either of the contending parties squarely at the door of the other, in a specified financial sense, and wants the party responsible for damage to rebuild the damaged places at their cost, and gets it also mutually agreed to by the parties.

These and other such case-histories may assist us in discovering the rationale and the roots of social behaviour. In the appraisal of the conflicts and tensions that are suggested through them the historian will have to be realistic; he should not overinterpret nor underplay the motives.

Archaeology can substantially help history in getting the bearings aright, to eliminate the *ad-hoc* treatment and the *status-quo* approach to a difficult situation or in the projection of the event retrospectively. Forces have worked for the acculturation, atrophy and degeneration of social structure from age to age. These have to be examined and identified.

2. Profile studies of societies—stable and sensitive areas

A profile study of societies on a regional basis, with regard to the cultural process should be documented on the basis of historical as well as archaeological evidence. The stable and the sensitive zones therein should be separately identified, and the rationale of the stability or sensitivity, as the case may be, should be defined.

3. Common basic legacy of the Indian citizen

The strength and weakness of various regional traditions in so far as they affect legal rights should be analysed, and spurious traditions exposed. Such a comprehensive cultural history of the functionally pivotal regions of India should be documented, in order, to bring out the common, positive and basic legacy (literary, cultural and ethnic), as had devolved from the archaeological into historical stages. This would indeed be the history that would strengthen regional identities with no detriment to a unitary identity. It cannot be gainsaid that the matrix of present Indian society was already formed in the early historic period and we should therefore give due importance to the study of Late Protohistorical archaeology. So far as this Protohistoric period is concerned, no satisfactory socio-economic and ethno-cultural theories have so far been acceptably framed. The period and its archaeological investigations are obviously fraught with serious and difficult issues. Unless and until corporate life in the Protohistoric and early historic stages is fully outlined, it would not be possible for any historian to draw objective conclusions on the basis of the retrospective claims of communities. The medieval period, in this respect, is relatively free from methodological difficulties.

Pilot studies should associate both the academic and the non-academic (traditional specialists of the cultural groups in the respective societies) so that an acceptable approach to the reconstruction of history may be made by a constructive dialogue on the debatable data. A carefully prepared questionnaire scheme might reveal the dimensions of the data available for historical reconstruction.

Transformed [illegible]

[illegible] as well as [illegible]. The step and [illegible] [illegible] of the [illegible]

2. Common Elements of [illegible]

[illegible]

[illegible]

Twenty Three

PURANIC APPROACH TO INDIAN HISTORY

A.B.L. AWASTHI

Itithasam Puravrittam Paramparyen-agatam

ITIHASA (cf. *Itihasa-Purana*) was a recognised subject in the ancient Indian corpus of learning. It was yoked to the Purana. Let us consider its importance for historical studies today.

Itihasa mainly denoted the *Ramayana* and the *Mahabharata*. Listening to itihasa-purana was considered an act of piety.

Itihasa literally means that which happened in the past (*iti ha asa*). Not ordinary events which had taken place were recorded but those of national importance which inspired people to do something good and great. History with its modern connotation is naturally the product of the modern age. The works of Kalhana, Jonaraja and others in the form of *Rajataranginis* as well as the *Rajavilasa* of Manakavi, a medieval work dealing with the history of Mewar on the pattern of Kalhana, partly connote history in the modern sense. The *Bhaktamala* of the poet Nabhadasa and the commentary of Priyadasa on it, is an important specimen of historical writing in medieval India. The Hathigumpha inscription of Kharavela of Kalinga is an impressive example of recording history in the modern sense of the term. Works of history, other than the Puranas, did exist until the time of Hsuan-tsang.[1] Temples and monasteries such as those at Nalanda, Vikramasila, Valabhi and Pushpagiri-Ratnagiri (In Orissa) were great centres of learning and had great libraries but the dust and ashes of the books burnt have disappeared. Others were lost owing to the ravages of time.

After the conquest of Sind by the Arabs styled *nastika saindhava yavana mlecchah*[2], the age of crisis—*yuganta*—began. The age of the Sultans of Delhi and the Mughuls was the age of the struggle for survival. In order to preserve the relics of the past the Puranas like the *Agni* and the *Garuda* began to give summaries of the *Ramayana*, the *Mahabharata*, the *Harivamsa*, the *Bhagvad-gita*, as well as of works on grammar, prosody, medicine, iconography etc. Sanskrit poets and artists began to use new symbolic terminology like the *gajasardula* (elephant-lion) *motif*.[3] Historical reference in the works of Tulsidas along the same lines have not been taken note of by modern historians.

With the advent of the modern age in India the unlocking of ancient sources began at the hands of European scholars. Comparative studies in languages led to the foundations of philology and comparative religion. Macdonnel, Maxmueller, Keith, Hopkins, Wilson, Kennedy, Buhler and Weber etc. made great contributions along these lines for the interpretation of Indian literature and tradition. Archaeology stepped in, and Marshall, Mackay, Fergusson, Cunningham, Stein and Prinsep etc. introduced new methods and opened new fields of historical studies. Many Indians like R.G. Bhandarkar, D.R. Bhandarkar, R.D. Bannerji, R.L. Mitra, R.P. Chanda, K.P. Jaiswal, D.R. Sahni, K.N. Dikshit and M.S. Vatsa etc. followed them. The great N.G. Mazumdar, died before his time in the service of history and archaeology.

Rapson and V.A. Smith emphasised the study of the Puranas. The former discussed the history of the Andhras (Satavahanas) in the light of the list of thirty rulers given in the Puranas in conjunction with their coins and inscriptions. I do not know if any body has added to Rapson's contribution.

When considering the Puranas, scholars, mostly base their views on Pargiter's *Dynasties of the Kali Age*. Recently Dr. Morton Smith tried to revise Pargiter's work with the help of archaeological data. But the product is un-balanced. The historical dynasties viz. Saisunagas, Nandas, Mauryas, Sungas, Andhras and Guptas have received very little attention. Even the historical gleanings from the Skanda Purana referring to important rulers and dynasties like Vikramaditya, Sudraka, Nanda, Budha (Gupta) and Pramiti (Dhanga) have not been utilised by scholars. Negligence of the Puranas and of Puranic researches is a sad commentary on the historiographical, if not the historical sense of the scholars of Indian history.

Let us see what new light the Puranas throw on the historical period beginning with the reign of Bimbisara.

Kakavarna

The Brihaddharma Purana refers to the reign of the king Kakavarna (Kakavarnakhyako-nripah) of Kikata desa or the Gaya desa *i.e.* Magadha[4], who was opposed to Brahmanas and the Brahmanical religion.[5] He is mentioned as a great atheist (*raja-parama-nastikah)*[6] and envious of Brahmanas (*Brahmadvesha-karastatha*)[7]. This is corroborated by the Buddhist sources which tell us that during the reign of Kakavarna-Kalasoka the second Buddhist council was held at Vaisali. He was the champion of Buddhism and apparently hostile to Brahmanas and Brahmanism.

Magadhaka Nandas

While describing the Janapadas of Prachya (East India), the Brahma Purana refers to the Nandas of Magadha (Magadhaka Nandas) who were none other than the Nanda rulers of Magadha uprooted by Chanakya and Chandragupta Maurya.

Dealing with the *Chaturyugi Vyavastha*, the Skanda Purana refers to Chanakya who destroyed the Nandas :

Tatsa trishu sahasreshu dasadhika satatrya bhavishyam
Nanda-rajyam cha Chanakyo yan hanishyati.

Chanakya himself asserts that the country and culture were liberated from the clutches of the Nandas by him.[10] This is supported by the *Mudrarakshasa.*[11]

Mauryas

From the beginning of our historical studies to this day the origin of the Mauryas has baffled historians who are not certain about it.

Even Dr. Radhakumud Mookerjee and Prof. C.D. Chatterji were not able to interpret correctly the terms *vrishala* and *Nandanavya* used for Chandragupta Maurya in the *Mudrarakshasa*.

The Puranas and the Mahabharata help us in solving the problem.

Sungas

Similarly the Sungas belonged to a tribe named Sunga mentioned in the Matsya Purana.[12] The term *audbhijja* used for Pushyamitra may also be interpreted with the help of the Puranas.

Raja Ghosha[13]

The *Ayodhya Mahatmya* of the *Skanda* Purana refers to Raja-Ghosha who is to be identified with his namesake, the son and successor of Pulindaka.

There is a reference to Raja Naravarman of Panchala[14] or Kanyakubja desa. Was he in any way connected with the king Yasovarman of Panchala of Kannauj?

It is my submission that there is an urgent need to prepare a new list of kings based on the Puranas and cull other types of material from this important source for a reconstruction of ancient Indian History. I have tried to achieve this aim partially in my *History from the Puranas*.

References

1. Saint Hilaire, Hiouen Thsang in India (Susil Gupta) 1952 Edn. p. 52.
2. Awasthi, *Garuda Purana-Eka Adhyayan,* pp 29-30.
3. Sculptures in the Rajarani temple and those at Konarka etc.
4. *Brihaddharma* P. 56.23 *Kakakarnakhyako* is a misprint for *Kakavarnakhyako*.

5. Ibid, 56,24-28
6. *op. cit*, 56.30
7. *op. cit*, 56.23
8. *Brahma P.* 27.53 (ii).
9. *Skanda P.* I (ii) 40.251
10. K. A. Shamasastry (1951) p. 463.
11. *Mudrarakshasa* I. 7.
12. *Matsya P.* (Jivanand, Calcutta, Edn. 1876), 143.41-42 (i) See A. B. L. Awasthi, *Prachina Bharat ka Itihasa.*
13. Studies in *Skanda Purana*, Pt. I
14. *Saura Purana* 48.29 : *Svayambhuve antare tvasidraja paramadharmikah, Panchala-vishaye vipra naravarmeti vishrutah.*

Twenty-Four

MODERN INDIA AND THE BENGAL SCHOOL OF HISTORY : A CRITIQUE

PRABHA DIXIT

A CAREFUL reading of the works of 20th century historians of Bengal would show that in spite of their different ideological commitments and their chronological placement, almost all of them, barring the economic historians, belong to one category as they display near-unanimity in their interpretation of certain aspects of Indian History as well as modern Bengal. This consensus is not imposed on them by historical evidence but stems from their blind love for Bengal and their obssessive admiration of the Bengali Hindu culture. Every ism—from sectarianism to Marxism—is harnessed to establish the cultural primacy of Bengal in the multi-dimensional growth of India that followed the British conquest. In their image-building variety of historiography the role of the non-Bengalis—both Hindu and Muslim—if not shown as directly or indirectly inspired by Bengal, either invites critical comments recorded in a most casual fashion or ignored altogether. For these historians, India that is not a magnified version of Bengal does not exist at all.

In more than one sense these historians restate, not with modifications but with embellishment, the self-view and the view of India which the Hindu intellectual reformers and political leaders of Bengal had held decades ago. Their attempt, simultaneously, to record and relive the past introduces a peculiar distortion in their perspective and makes them parochial in their outlook. R.C. Majumdar candidly admits as much when he writes : "Bengal is now dead, and ghosts and goblins are now dancing over her mutilated corpse. But Bengal will live in history long after those who now strut on the political stage of India have passed into obloquy or oblivion. Some day perhaps, that history will be written. In the meantime I leave this booklet as the epitaph on the grave of that is no more".[1] A serious student of Indian History, who is familar with the developments and contributions made by the other regions and communities of India, would regard the exaggerated claims of Bengali historians as nothing but glorification of the past because they are despaired of their present and are doubtful about the future. Professor Susobhan Sarkar virtually echoes the sentiments expressed by Majumdar : "The impact of British rule, bourgeois economy and modern western culture was felt first in Bengal and produced an awakening known usually as the Bengal Renaissance ...... In the broad family of peoples which constitute India, the recognition of the distinctiveness of the Bengalis has been in modern times largely bound up with the appreciation of this flowering of social, religious, literary and political activities in Bengal. And today when distintegration threatens every aspect of our life, it is more necessary than ever to recall our past heritage, to go over again the struggles and achievements which had built up a proud tradition now in danger of being forgotton".[2] For the Bengali historians, thus, past is not an object of investigation, it is an escape route that guarantees protection of their ego and preservation of their pride.

In a plural society, unfortunately, histories of regions or communities, written under such intellectual compulsions create unwarranted distances and competitions which hamper their integration and promote feelings that may lead to break up of an established nation. They are more dangerous than those which make religion the sole denominator of progress or decline of a nation. That is so because they promote two sets of rivalries simultaneously—inter-regional and inter-religious.

Some of the most glaring examples reflecting the cultural chauvinism, parochialism and communalism of Bengali historians are discussed below to expose the uncritical and highly biased character of their historiography.

The social and cultural changes in 19th century Bengal are viewed by the Bengali historians as unique events which gave birth to Bengal renaissance and made Bengal the cultural leader of the rest of the people of this country. With great pride Sir Jadunath Sarkar tells us, "Bengal became a path-finder and a light-bringer to the rest of India. If Periclean Athens was the school of hellas, the eyes of Greece, mother of arts and eloquence, that was Bengal to the rest of India under the British rule. In this new Bengal originate every good and great thing of Modern World that passed on to the other provinces of India. From Bengal went forth the English educated teachers and the European inspired thought that helped to modernize Bihar and Orissa, Hindustan and Daccan".[3]

In spite of his Marxian commitment Susobhan Sarkar could not rise above his loyalty to Bengal. In his view "the role played by Bengal in the modern awakening of India is comparable to the position occupied by Italy in the history of the European Renaissance".[4]

In a vast country like ours, no single person or province has ever succeeded in becoming the Guru—Superior for others in the sphere of culture. Nor has the cultural exchange between two regions ever resulted in the merger of their separate identities. Upto the close of 18th century, cultural exchange between the elites of two different regions was an established practice. But after the British conquest this tradition underwent a sea-change. Inter-regional and inter-communal cultural borrowing was replaced by nearly one-way traffic with Europe. The socio-cultural developments in each region, manifested, in varying degrees, a pattern which was very similar to that of Bengal. The credit for these developments, however, does not go to Bengal; it goes to the British imperialists who introduced mini-scale modernisation to serve their own mundane interests. The English-educated Indians and their non-technical western education were essential parts of that process. The political aspirations and the cultural dilemma of the early generations of educated Indians achieved a uniform character throughout the country because they stemmed from a common origin.

Following the tradition of 19th century thinkers, the Bengali historians regard the pre-British non-industrial India as degenerate and implicitly consider the British domination as the most fortuitous event without which progress of this country would have remained unrealised.

"It was indeed the darkest period in modern Indian history. Old society and polity had crumbled and the ruins of an old social order lay scattered on all sides. As yet there was no force which could clear the debris and there was no attempt to rebuild on the ancient foundations. Dead traditions, fossilised customs and irrational bigotry had choked the life-stream of the nation. Knowledge had been lost. It was a period of unrelenting darkness .. The battle of Plassey had already sealed the fate of Bengal... and in spite of the prevailing chaos, the shape of the new order of things was emerging slowly. The West, heralded by Britain, had come to India not merely as an agent of commerce, but as an instrument of history, destined to shake India out of her stupor and to release a new tide of thought and activity in the old river-bed of history."[5] The British undertook this Herculean task and the result was the so-called renaissance in Bengal.

On this criterion, even today, after two centuries of British rule and the regeneration accomplished by the Bengali reformers, the vast majority of our people continue to live in a degenerate state. They are illiterate, poor, ignorant and superstitious. This suggests two things: either no regeneration took place, or, we were not degenerate but held only a radically different world-view and bases of social organisation than those of the British rulers. Political instability and static culture are not sure symptoms of degeneration. They may well indicate only a point of transition in the growth of a society. Carrying the argument a step further, these historians should also reject Gandhi's concept of village India as an evil to be abhorred and launch a crusade against all Indian intellectuals and leaders engaged in the work of national reconstruction on the lines suggested by him.

This desperate search for the European industrial culture in 19th century India and condemnation of Indian people for not possessing it as displayed in the works of Bengali historians shows a total lack of perspective on their part and exposes the uncritical style of their writing. Further, if rejection of pre-British culture was a step forward then how could revival of that very culture after a quarter century infuse new life in Hindu Society? Did not Bankimchandra and Vivekananda propagate a socio-cultural philosophy that was the reverse of Raja Rammohan Roy's?

In the face of the grandeur of "resurgent Bengal", these historians become oblivious to the simple truth of history that no people have ever succeeded in achieving regeneration under an alien rule. In comparing Bengal with Greece or Italy, no note is taken of the political state of its society. Italy of the renaissance or Germany of the reformation remained politically disintegrated and culturally backward till the middle of 19th century. The culture of Greece when imported by independent countries led to the flowering of their genius, yet after losing its independence to the Ottoman Turks that very culture could not save Greece from sliding into ignorance and superstition. Grafting does not succeed on dead wood nor can it rejuvenate a tree whose roots have withered. That India could rise again and liberate herself from the foreign yoke is proof that British imperialism did not confront an inert society and a lifeless culture. It was face to face with a politically disintegrated pre-industrial society only. That is why the grafting of western culture by them bore fruits of a variety not desired by them.

The thought process that makes these historians regard 19th century India a period of darkness is also responsible for their denial to accept the uprising of 1857 as a popular revolt by the Indians against alien rulers. Dr. R.C. Majumdar starts with an apologia : "At the very outset it is very necessary to emphasise the fact that in the absence of all records from the Indian side-sepoys as well as their so-called leaders—the evidence so far available to us cannot be regarded as sufficient nor of such nature as would enable us to arrive at any definite and final conclusion on this subject...".[6] Having said this he immediately proceeds to do just the opposite. He emphatically states: "The miseries and bloodshed of 1857-58 were not the birth-pangs of freedom movement in India, but the dying groans of an obsolete aristocracy and centrifugal feudalism of the medieval age".[7] This conclusion is based on the grounds that the uprising of 1857 had no recognised leaders, no conspiracy, no common goal, no universal support and it did not spread to the whole of India but remained confined to its northern parts. Further, the landed gentry, commercial classes as well as educated Indians vehemently opposed it and cooperated with the British to suppress the rebels. Being merely "anti-British in character, it cannot be termed either as national or freedom movement."[8] S.B. Chaudhuri skirts the alternate characterization of 1857 revolt as suggested by R.C. Majumdar by emphasizing the role of the civil population in the great upheaval. He writes: "The question whether the mutiny was a mere military revolt or popular uprising when calmly considered leads to the conclusion that the army revolted, the population left to itself committed overt acts of hostility against the Government. This is rebellion ... the revolt of that year appears to have been the first combined attempt of many classes of people to challenge a foreign power. This is a real, if remote approach to the freedom movement of India of a later stage"[9].

The civilians who participated in the revolt, according to these historians, were not inspired by "patriotism" but "by selfish motives". They were "riff-raffs", "anti-social elements" who formed the "scum of society" who are always on the forefront to take advantage of political anarchy. Their twisted logic does not permit them to accept any evidence favourable to the rebels. They want us to believe that being "anti-British" and not for India's liberation made the uprising of 1857 a reactionary movement whose failure was a blessing in disguise for this country. That the cry of 1857 rebels "*Firingi vapas Jao*" (Europeans go back) might have been the prototype of the nationalist slogan of *"Angrezo Bharat Chhodo"* (British, Quite India) in 1942 is a possibility which these historians do not consider worthy of their objective investigation.

In this connection it will be but apt to ask them why the same criterion is not applied in assessing the character of the Swadeshi movement of Bengal in 1905 ? Did not the entire Muslim community, the low caste Hindus, the people of Bihar, Orissa and Assam, the aristocracy as well as a vast majority of educated Indians keep aloof from this movements. Why should this movement, in favour of reunification of a province, be termed as "freedom struggle" when freedom of India was not on its agenda? Were not the vested interests of the educated Bengali Hindus adversely affected by this division? On what grounds may the interests of this section of Bengali population be regarded superior to those which were at the base of the revolt of 1857?

But logic does not seem to be the strong point of Bengali historians. While obliquely justifying Bengal's support to the British during the testing times of the Mutiny, they condemn Maharaja Ranjit Singh, the Lion of the Punjab, for not challenging the British might. They also dub the Marathas as marauders though they valiantly fought the British for nearly a century.

The boundary line of pre-partition India for the Bengali historian is conterminous with their home province. In recording the developments in modern India they keep themselves confined to Bengal and seldom stray into other regions. Narrating the march of Indian History through the ages Sir Jadunath Sarkar gets stuck in Bengal when he comes to the modern period. Except the Arya Samaj, which is dismissed in a puny paragraph of 11 lines, no non-Bengali movement finds a place in his book.[10] Similarly, National Education, for Haridas and Uma Mukherjee means exclusively the programme of education outlined by Satish Chandra Mukherjee and the activities of the Dawn society. The Bhagwat Chatushpathi founded in 1897 is viewed by them as an important part of the National Education although its declared aims do not justify such categorisation. Its object was "to enable all willing persons to study Hindu religion, philosophy and other Hindu Sastras according to the ancient orthodox method, under able and experienced teachers free of charge"[11]. The programme of national education launched by the Hindus of the Punjab which led to the foundation of the D.A.V. College at Lahore and the Gurukul at Kangri, or the Deoband seminary established to impart religious education to the Muslims are excluded from their account of national education. But when they come to Bankim Chandra and Vivekananda the historians of Bengal instantly assume the role of hagiographers. Both are the much eulogized fathers of the Indian nation, prophets of modern India and saviours of the Hindu religion. It is stated that Vivekananda was : "A high priest of national resurgence, a prophet of socialist order..." "In him... Hinduism was reborn as an aggressive and dynamic religion..." His triumphant career in America "raised Indian nationalism to the higest peak of glory by giving Hinduism, for the first time, a prominent place in the cultural map of the world, and he also placed nationalism on a high spiritual level"[12].

The reality behind the myths woven around these figures, however, point towards another direction. The verbal duel between the East and West had been initiated much earlier by the European scholars themselves. They took pains to assign different missions to the different nations of the world to avoid duplication in the work of regeneration of mankind. The mission assigned to India was that of spirituality, while the preservation of material culture was to be in the main the "burden of the white man". The poor Hindu peasants could not draw any sustenance from Vivekananda's spiritual message. It could not help them to resist the exploitation of the Zamindars of Bengal or the moneylenders of the Punjab.

The Indian nation and people of Bengal as depicted in the writings of Bengali historians do not include the Muslim community unless they are to be blamed for the degeneration of the Hindus. Raja Rammohan Roy, who served as the *vakil* of the last Mughal Emperor Bahadur Shah Zafar was the first to enunciate this thesis. He wrote : "The country having been so long under subjection to the arbitrary military government of the Mohammedan rulers, which showed little respect for Hindu learning, it has very much decayed and indeed almost disappeared, except among the Brahmans in some parts of the Dakhan, and of the eastern side of India, more distant from the chief seat of Mohammedan government".[13] With a feeling of gratefulness he also pointed out that : "The greater part of Hindustan having been for several centuries subject to Mohammedan Rule, the civil and religious rights of its original inhabitants were constantly trampled upon, and from the habitual oppression of the conquerors, a great body of their subjects in the southern Peninsula, afterwards called Marattahs, and another body in the western parts now styled Sikhs, were at last driven to revolt; and when the Mussulman power became feeble, they ultimately succeeded in establishing their independence; but the natives of Bengal wanting in vigour of body and adverse to active exertion, remained during the whole period of Muhammedan conquest, faithful to the existing government, although their property was often plundered, their religion insulted and their blood wantonly shed. Divine Providence at last, in its abundant mercy, stirred up the English nation to break the yoke of those tyrants, and to receive the oppressed natives of Bengal under its protection".[14]

When not castigated for their religious fanaticism, the Muslims are made the target of contemptuous indifference. Their existence is completely ignored.[15] Describing the position of the Hindus in Bengal, Sir Jadunath Sarkar points out, "...between 1830 and 1870, the Hindus not only recovered the ground that they had lost during the six centuries of orthodox Muslim rule, but forged ahead in wealth, culture and share in the administration".[16]

All Muslim movements are branded as anti-national and their leaders described as collaborators of British imperialism. The continuation of the British connection desired by a Bipin Chandra Pal or a Surendra Nath Bannerjea at a time when Indian's had launched their non-co-operation movement under Mahatma Gandhi, or the Hindu nationalism of Aurobindo, does not make them anti-national or communal. No attempt is made to adequately explain the reasons for the non-participation of the Muslims in the Swadeshi agitation.[17] The standard explanation of this vital question runs as follows: The "pro-Muslim policy of the British Government...the extensive campaigning of the *Mullahs* and *Maulvis* of Bengal as well as the keen desire of the all India Muslim Leaders of Aligarh to defend and safeguard their communal interests against the Hindus was responsible for it".[18] The role of the Hindu leaders is never critically examined. The fact that the doors of the Hindu College, Calcutta, were not open to the Muslims or that no Muslim could even become a member of a terrorist organization are of no consequence to these historians.

The main fault of the Muslims, according to Sir Jadunath Sarkar was: "The Indian Muslims have throughout the succeeding centuries, retained the extra-Indian direction of their hearts. Their faces are still turned, in daily prayer, to a spot in Mecca; before English education modernised India, their minds, their law code, their administrative system, their reading sought models from outside India — from Arabia and Syria, Persia and Eygpt".[19] But the great Bengali historian completely forgot that he himself was looking not only towards Europe but also drawing inspiration from it. What is worse, he even eulogized the enslavement of India by the British because thereby the Hindus got liberated after "six centuries of alien domination".[20]

The Bharatiya Vidya Bhawan historiography, commonly mistaken as the intellectual version of Veer Savarkar's political ideology is, in fact, a product of the Bengali school of historiography. Sample a quotation from Sir Jadunath Sarkar. He writes in *Shivaji and his times*: "He (Shivaji) has proved that the Hindu race can still produce not only *jamadars* (non-commissioned officers) and *chitnises* (clerks), but also rulers of men, and even a king of kings (Chhatrapati). The Emperor Jaghangir cut the *Akshay Bat* tree of Allahabad down to its roots and hammered a red-hot iron cauldron on its stump. He flattered himself that he had killed it. But lo ! within a year the tree began to grow again and pushed the heavy obstruction to its growth aside".

"Shivaji has shown that the tree of Hinduism is not really dead, that it can rise from beneath the seemingly crushing load of centuries of political bondage, exclusion from the administration and legal repression; it can put forth new leaves and branches; it can again lift its head up to the skies".[21]

The short spell of glory which the educated Hindus of Bengal enjoyed as a result of a capsulized modernization of India in 19th century cannot keep the major portion of Indian History fettered to the *Sonar Bangla* of their dreams. The contributions made by the other regions in the making of modern India cannot be excluded from national history to preserve the illusion of the past granduer that haunts the minds of the Bengali intellectuals, including historians. The taste of parochialism, whether intellectual or practical, can never be sweet. The slogan 'Bengal for the Begalis' glorified in the Swadeshi agitation when repeated by the neighbours sounds crude and unpleasant to Bengali ears. Provoked by one of such utterances Dr. R.C. Majumdar lashed out in the dedication of one of his books: "Dedicated To the Memory OF BENGAL THAT WAS by one Who Has The Misfortune To Live In BENGAL THAT IS While The CROAKING AHOM FROGS Kicked With Impunity The DYING BENGAL ELEPHANT And the PEOPLE AND GOVERNMENT OF INDIA Merely Looked ON."[22]

In short, except for the historians dealing with ancient India,[23] Bengal has mainly produced either chroniclers or hagiographers whose sights seldom cross the boundaries of Bengal and within Bengal rarely notice the existence of the non-Bengalis as well as the non-Hindus.

References

1. Mujumdar, R.C., *Glimpses of Bengal in the Nineteenth Century* Calcutta, 1960, preface.
2. Sarkar, Susobhan : also see Sen, A. *Bengal Renaissance and Other Essays,* Calcutta, 1970, pp. 3-4.

3. Sarkar, J. N. : *History of Bengal,* Vol. II Reprint, Patna, 1973, p. 498.
4. Sen, Amit (pseudonym of Susobhan Sarkar) : *Notes on the Bengal Renaissance,* Calcutta, 1967, p. 1.
   Also see Nemai Sadhan Bose, *The Indian Awakening and Bengal,* (Second edition), Calcutta, 1969, ; preface and Susobhan Sarkars's *Bengal Renaissance and Other Essays,* Delhi, 1970, p. 3.
5. Tagore, Saumyendra Nath : *Raja Rammohun Roy,* New Delhi, 1966, pp. 7-8.
6. Mujumdar, R. C. : *Sepoy Mutiny, 1857*, Calcutta, 1957, p. 214.
7. Majumdar, R. C. : *op. cit.* p. 241 ; Sen, S.N. *Eighteen Fifty Seven*, Publications Division, Government of India 1957. Chattopadhyay, H., *Sepoy Mutiny 1857*, Calcutta, 1957.
   Besides these monographs, other works also support this view.
8. See Mujumdar, R. C. : *Sepoy Mutiny, 1857.*
9. Chaudhuri, S.B. : *Civil Rebellion In the Indian Mutinies,* Calcutta, 1957, pp. 287-297.
10. Sarkar, J.N. : *India Through the Ages*, Calcutta, 1926, pp. 66-74.
11. Mukherjee, Hari Das and Uma : *The Origins of National Education,* Calcutta, 1957, p. 12.
12. Majumdar, R.C., *Glimpses of Bengal in the 19th Century*, Calcutta, 1960, p. 77 ; Mukherjee, Hari Das and Uma, *op cit.*, p. 214, also see their *Bande Mataram and the Indian Nation*, Calcutta, 1957., Bose, Nemai Sadhan, *op. cit.* p. 164. There is an interminably long list of authors who write in the same vein ; Bose, A.N. in *Studies in Bengal Renaissance,* A. C. Gupta (ed.) Calcutta, 1958, p. 105 ; Ray, N.R., in *History of Bengal*, N.K. Sinha (ed.) Calcutta, 1957, p. 179 ; Dutta, K.K. *Renascent India,* Calcutta, 1976, pp, 130-42 ; Ghosal, H.R. *An Outline History of the Indian People*, Govt. of India, Publications Division, 1968, p. 165 ; Mitra, Hara Prasad, *Vivekanander Jatiya O Samajik Chintan,* Calcutta, 1968, Basu, S.P., *Vivekananda O Samkaleen Bharatvarsha*, Calcutta, 1965.
13. *Selected Works of Raja Rammohan Roy,* Delhi, 1977, p. 80.
14. *op cit.*, pp. 98-99.
15. Ghoshal H.R. ; *An Outine History of the Indian People,* Government of India, Publications Division, 1968. Ghose, Jotirmoy *Banglar Sanskriti Oltihasa* Calcutta, 1975. Majumdar, M., *Banglar Nabjug,* Calcutta, 1975.
16. *India through the Ages,* p. 92.
17. Sumit Sarkar's *Swadeshi Movement in Bengal,* Calcutta, 1973, is an exception in this regard.
18. Mukherjee, Hari Das and Uma : *India's Fight for Freedom,* p. 252.
19. Sarkar, Jadunath : *India Through the Ages*, 4th edition, Calcutta, 1960, p. 41.
20. Sarkar, Jadunath : *Fall of the Mughal Empire,* Vol. 4 (revised edition) Calcutta, 1950. p. 347.

21. Sarkar, Jadunath : *Shivaji and his times*, Delhi, 1973, pp. 389-90; also see Sen, S.N. : *Administrative system of the Marathas,* 3rd edition, Calcutta, 1976, preface and p. iii.
22. See his *Glimpses of Bengal in the 19th Century.*
23. It has just been brought to my notice that this period too suffers from a similar approach. One example cited is a special appendix by Prof. R. C. Majumdar on *The death of Rajyavardhana (Classical Age* pp. 121-3) to absolve the Bengali king Sasanka, atleast of the likely treachery involved in his murder of Rajyavardhana of Thanesar.

22. [illegible]

23. [illegible]

BATTLE FOR THE PAST

D.P. SINGHAL

> The Historian without his facts is rootless and futile; the facts without their historian are dead and meaningless ... [History] is a continuous process of interaction between the historian and his facts, an unending dialogue between the present and the past.
>
> E.H. Carr, *What is History*, p. 24.

IN RECENT years, a number of publications of uneven quality have come out on Indian history. The writers include a wide variety of historians, professional or politically committed, and pseudo-historians, journalists or courtiers, expressing their respective attitudes and approaches. While many of these narratives are works of history, some, not unexpectedly, are inspired by nationalistic feelings, aiming at emphasising the evils of the colonial past and the virtues of the pre-colonial era ; or by ideological commitment, subordinating intellectual freedom to political objectives and denouncing India's cultural past as a hindrance to economic advancement; or by communalist beliefs, looking at history in terms of religious tensions and conflicts.

In Britain, too, a great deal of historical activity relating to India has emerged, concentrating on what was regarded as the good record of the British colonial rule ; or taking a nostalgic look at the "brightest jewel in the imperial crown"; or even defending the imperialist rule in toto by characterising it as a harbinger of modernisation.

Ideologically committed or inspired scholars seek to reinterpret India's past, aiming not so much at unfolding and explaining happenings in history as at employing the past to support change in the course of history. People derive immense pride and courage from the knowledge of the great deeds of their past and achievements of their ancestors. Consequently, the major battle for the past begins between those who overrate the importance and value of their historical inheritance and those who underrate or deride it. Both are trading in half-truths. However, these patriotic and ideological attitudes are important as they provide the inspiration for writing history, but to accept them as the sole or even dominating motive force in rewriting Indian history would be misleading.

The need for re-writing history arises from a variety of reasons and new interpretations are not necessarily tendentious. For example, if an Indian historian criticises a British historian, or a non-Marxist disagrees with a Marxist or a pseudo-Marxist, why should it be a difference between two nationalities or two ideologies, and not a dispute between two historians? It is true that sometimes it is not possible to separate the historicity of the historian from his ideological commitment, or his individual eccentricity from his group-consciousness. For, an historian is as much a political man as he is a professional being.

Yet history has been sufficiently used as an effective instrument of "brain washing" to deserve periodic accusations of partisanship. Historians who are seduced from truth and who stoop to distorting facts for a certain end do not necessarily assert what is absolutely false. As all questions in politics are questions of comparison and degree and in every human transaction there is a mixture of good and evil, it is possible to make a saint appear a tyrant or vice versa by assembling half-truths dexterously and applying searching scepticism to the evidence on one side, and credulity to the other.

Historical investigation is an unending process. Historians hardly ever agree on interpretation, but they generally admit the need for each generation to re-write history. Yet every historian claims to be telling the truth, as no one else has done before, and points out the errors of inconsistencies, of omissions, and of assumptions, in the writings of his predecessors. This can only be explained—if national or ideological bias is not involved—by realising that history is not the re-enactment of the past, but a recollection of it. The involvement of the element of human perception in recording events and interpreting them makes historical narratives, even when based on the same data, so varied. Hence a discovery of new material, a change in outlook, values or society brought about by a revolution or advancement of knowledge, must lead to re-writing of history. Indian history is no exception. The changing concepts of history alone require periodic revisions. History is not what it was a few centuries ago ; it certainly has travelled a long way from the scrupulous cataloguing of events to the tracing of their causal links.

History, therefore, is what historians make of it and claims to, Complete objectivity must remain untenable, as must Lord Acton's hope, that histories of such impartiality can be written, that can be accepted as satisfactory by every possible reader, whatever his race or creed. Even Marxist historians, who claim that history can be a science and deny the importance of the subjective role of the historian, admit that there is an element of truth in the relativity of the study of history to the historian. History is subjective, however, only to the extent it carries the stamp of its writer's personality. So long as the story is allowed to unfold itself naturally, without any deliberate distortion or suppression of facts, it is historically an objective account, irrespective of the conclusions drawn. Once the narrative is geared to an objective, or personal bias is replaced by group-prejudice, it is at once reduced to propaganda. Writing history, therefore, is a task requiring high moral standards, as well as high intellectual capabilities. An academic historian must, to the best of his capacity, sink into and absorb the past by acquiring all the knowledge possible for the particular period or topic or region he is studying. He must neglect nothing and remain keenly aware of the gaps that remain. His task is one of selection and comprehension—selecting from an incomplete but vast mass of static records the dynamic and living reality that once was life and then forming from that selection an account of the past that is at once both less and more significant than the past itself. Since history deals with living and changing human beings, the hardest task of the historian is to recognise and signalize every change as it comes. Small wonder Oscar Wilde said, "Anybody can make history; only a great man can write it".

The ancient period of India, with all its wealth of rich literary sources, is conspicuous for its lack of historical texts. Ancient India did not produce a Thucydides, but there is considerable evidence to suggest that every important Hindu court maintained archives and geneologies of its rulers. And Kalhana's *Rajatarangini*, written in twelfth century Kashmir, is a remarkable piece of historical literature. Despite his lapses into myths and legends, Kalhana had an unbiased approach to historical facts and history writing. He held that a true historian, while recounting the events of the past, must discard love (*raga*) and hatred *(dvesha)*. Indeed, his well-developed concept of history and the technique of historical investigation have given rise to some speculation that there existed at the time a powerful tradition of historiography in which Kalhana must have received his training.

The Muslim rulers during the medieval period had a keener sense of history, but it did not stretch much beyond giving an account of royal courts, households, military campaigns and religious activities. The history of Hindu society and its culture was generally neglected. A clear chronology of the major political events is certainly established, but little is known of the changing patterns of society. It was not until the expansion of Western knowledge in India that there emerged historians who, trained in scientific techniques of historical investigation, began to explore their own past.

It was, however, the British who first began to investigate the heritage of India and who laid the foundations of Indian history. The first comprehensive history of India, *History of British India* (1818), was attempted by the utilitarian thinker, James Mill, who naturally assumed the superiority of the British over India and its past. Highly selective in his evidence, he declared that the people of Europe, even during the feudal ages, were greatly superior to the Hindus, and denied that India had reached a high degree of civilization during the ancient period, even though the work of Sir William Jones and other European scholars had by then unearthed a volume of evidence to the contrary. Having indicted Indian society, he advocated the use of power and law to revolutionize it.

Despite the European discovery of India's past greatness and well-developed civilization, the British, having become the paramount power in India, remained generally convinced of their own superiority over Indians, and continued to feed themselves on Mill and Macaulay, who held Indians and their literature in low esteem and sought to create "black Englishmen" in India. Even Edmund Burke's philosophical conservatism asserting the supremacy of Indian traditions and his criticism of the British "drain" of Indian wealth made no lasting impression on the British mind. They insisted on accepting the degenerate conditions of the eighteenth century India as its normal condition, looked upon their rule as part of the perennial struggle between West and East, between liberty and despotism, and characterised it as "the march of civilization", in which authoritarianism and political power were employed to dethrone "oriental despotism" to ensure the growth of civilized communities. Seeley declared that nothing as great was ever done by Englishmen as the conquest of India, which was "not in the ordinary sense a conquest at all", and which he put on a par "with the Greek conquest of the East", pointing out that the British who had a "higher and more vigorous civilization than the native races" founded the Indian Empire "...partly out of a philanthropic desire to put an end to enormous evils" of the "robber-states of India". Even before such a moral basis had been given to British rule in India and the doctrines of guardianship or of trusteeship had evolved, popular historians such as Macaulay and Malleson had sought to explain the British ascendancy in terms of the superiority of British individual or national character. Either the remarkable qualities of people like Clive and Hastings or the inherent virtues of the British race were held responsible for British triumphs. A Western scholar, Bearce, observed in a recent study :

> Only prejudice and rather shallow thinking could have led men to suppose that they were superior to their fellow men, that military success had enduring value, and that Britain could rule India better than Indians.
>
> (From G.D. Bearce, *British Attitudes Towards India*, p. 301.)

Not all British historians reacted favourably to Mill. Elphinstone, in his *History of Hindu and Muhammadan India* (1839), though cautious and somewhat hesitant, took a more favourable view of Indian history. While not disagreeing with the general political approach of the British to India, Hunter criticized Mill and attempted to present the cultural past of India more sympathetically. He did not deny British superiority, but wanted the British rule to rest on goodwill and to change the Indian society with the cooperation of the people.

While utilitarian thought impressed the need to assert supremacy of law on the "uncultivated society" of India, and encouraged the claims to praise Britain as the creator of Indian prosperity, culminating in the writings of historians such as Seeley, the rise of Liberalism and Marxism led to the development of ideas and movements which were opposed to political subordination and economic disparity and which attributed the alarmingly increasing impoverishment of India to British rule. Of the scholars who pointed out that India's wealth was being drained by Britain, and who initiated the study of the economic history of India in a systematic way, three are most important. They were all non-Marxists and they published their studies at about the same time. They were William Digby, who published his *Prosperous British India* in 1901; Dadabhai Naoroji who published his *Poverty and Un-British Rule in India* in 1901 ; and R.C. Dutt, who published volume one of his *The Economic History of India* in 1902, and volume two in 1904. This was the heyday of British imperialism.

At the same time, Hobson in his book *Imperialism* (1902), starting from the liberal standpoint, demonstrated that the motive behind the expansion of the British rule abroad was the capitalist necessity of investing surplus capital abroad.

Between 1853 and 1857, Marx wrote twenty-three articles on India, and Engels eight, exposing British rule in India. Marx took what has been recently described as a "Europe-centred" view of India's past and saw in British rule a "double mission to India", one destructive, and the other regenerating. Britain was to lay the foundations of the material progress in India on the annihilation of the traditional Indian society. He wrote in 1853:

> Indian society has no history at all, at least no known history. What we call its history, is but the history of the successive intruders who founded their empires on the passive basis of that unresisting and unchanging society. The question, therefore, is not whether the English had a right to conquer India, but whether we are to prefer India conquered by the Turk, by the Persian, by the Russian, to India conquered by the Briton.
>
> England has to fulfil a double mission in India: One destructive, and the other regenerating—the annihilation of old Asiatic society, and the laying of the material foundations of Western society in Asia.
>
> Arabs, Turks, Tartars, Moguls, who had successively overrun India, soon became Hinduised, the barbarian conquerors being, by an eternal law of history, conquered themselves by the superior civilization of their subjects. The British were the first conquerors. Superior, and therefore inaccessible to Hindu civilization. They destroyed it by breaking up the native communities, by uprooting the native industry, and by levelling all that was great and elevated in the native society. The historic pages of their rule in India report hardly anything beyond that destruction. The work of regeneration hardly transpires through a heap of ruins. Nevertheless, it has begun.[1]

Marxist historians have carried on Marx's view of Indian history—denunciation of the Indian cultural heritage, as well as of British imperial rule in India.

Ignoring the concepts of economic exploitation of India, British nationalist/imperialist historians, such as Valentine Chirol, Vincent Smith, Dodwell, Coupland and others, continued to write at the beginning of this century more or less in the same strain as Seeley, making it abundantly clear that India was merely a geographical expression, and would relapse into its old state of degeneration if the firm hand of the benevolent paramount power was withdrawn. "Take away the British raj", said Lord Bryce, "and the idea of unity will vanish like morning mist". The unifying influence of Hindu culture was not even considered. Nationalism in India was generally ignored or heavily underestimated. At best, the Indian national movement was an agitation on the part of some disgruntled elite, including lawyers and the professional people, who sought high administrative positions and political power for themselves. In fact, they implied that the British Government was protecting the interests of the Indian masses against the elitist and self-seeking Indian nationalists. Vincent Smith in his famous and widely read *Oxford History of India* did not mention the Indian National Congress and its demands, even though the Congress had become by then a major factor in Indian politics. He accepted autocracy as the normal form of government in India and did not mention republicanism as it was known to ancient India. Verney Levett in his *Cambridge History of India* made no distinction between crime and revolutionary national agitation. When Indian nationalism could no longer be ignored, it was described as the sole product of European liberalism, British policy and English education. Those British writers who took a sympathetic attitude towards India were run down as wicked "radicals" or "sentimentalists" who hampered the "good work of ruling India".

This attitude continued even after Indian Independence. India was thrown into the British lap in a state of absent-mindedness ; the British had given India unity, order and modernisation, and the declining, even decadent, Indian civilization was superseded by a superior culture. Percival Spear's *India—A Modern History*, is a fine example of this. It must be pointed out, however, that the style of a modern Smith had to be remodelled and made agreeable to suit the changed Indo-British political relationship. Today it is not possible for a writer, who desires to be listened to, to speak as frankly and boldly as Smith could fifty years ago, or Seeley could ninety years ago, or as some other imperialist historians before him. Spear's book, as that of Seeley, reflects scholarship but not an understanding of India and gives a distorted picture of the Indian people and their heritage. Unlike Seeley, he does not expound that the British acquired India out of a philanthropic desire to put an end to the enormous evils of the "robber-states of India", although he stresses clearly the anarchy prevalent at the time, and while unlike James Mill, he is not contemptuous of Hindu India, he still depicts Hinduism as containing superstitions and evil institutions. More subtly than Smith, Dodwell and Coupland, he implies that the British conquest was beneficial for the Indians, and whatever good they have today is the outcome of its impact on their society.

India, as the British found it in the eighteenth century, was in a state of utter degeneration, but it was certainly not its permanent condition. Indian civilization has a long, continuous and glorious ancestry and, all historians now agree, that even at its earliest known period, it gave evidence of maturity, vitality and tolerance. It was a healthy society inhabited by a virile and vigorous people, who while "accepting joys and burdens of life, were ever searching for the ultimate and the universal". Their contributions in the spheres of art, language, philosophy, and science were remarkable and they bequeathed to humanity the *Upanishads*, the Buddha and the system of decimal notation. Their political and social institutions were very advanced for their time and they were famous for their republics, hospitals and universities. Their metaphysics and mathematics and medical science had considerably influenced contemporary civilizations and attracted world-wide attention. But Spear dilutes the effect of this vitality by making only brief and casual reference to such themes. In contrast, he gives a fresh lease to the old distorted image of India by referring repeatedly and at considerable length to features such as racial diversity, territorial disunity, rigid religious rituals and decadent social institutions.

It was inevitable that reaction against such partisan historiography should set in, especially during the period of national consciousness. New ideas and movements were increasingly captivating the Indian mind and Indians, scholars and others alike, had found new courage to defend themselves against undeserved onslaughts which until recently they had been content to ignore. Intense emotions of national pride produced at times equally extreme views, whose historicity, however, was somewhat tenuous. They upheld the supremacy of their own culture and civilization and tried to belittle the Western contribution. Hinduism was defended in its entirety, and certain of its ardent advocates even asserted its supremacy over other religions. Social abuses, such as the caste system were either denied or diluted or rationalised. Even Sati was in some ways glorified. The British regime was denounced as rooted in tyranny and exploitation ; their military successes were attributed either to treachery, forgery or bribery. Whatever be the verdict on the historicity of such writings, many of them were based upon sound historical research and had given a new impetus to Indian scholars to scientifically investigate their own past for themselves. Writers, such as Dadabhai Naoroji, R. Dutt, Major Basu, Savarkar, Tilak and others, can thus be justifiably regarded as forerunners of modern Indian historiography.

As a reaction against the Indian nationalism which emphasised democracy and pride in the culture of the past, which in turn meant the majority rule of the Hindus, and the dominance of Hindu culture, there developed Muslim communalism. To give itself political cohesion, it emphasised the importance of religion and mutual antagonisms between Hinduism and Islam. I.H. Qureshi, a noted historian and a Muslim League leader is an excellent example of this school of thought. He was an ardent advocate of Muslim separatism. Putting his ideas in an historical perspective, in his *The Muslim Community of the Indo-*

Pakistani Sub-Continent (610-1947): An Historical Analysis (The Hague, 1962), he unfolded the story of Indian Muslims in terms of religious conflict. Islam spread in India, he maintained, through persuasion, not coercion, and because of its supremacy over Hinduism. British domination of India was brought about by the meek submission of the Hindus, and misdeeds of the unorthodox Muslim sects, such as Shias and Ismailis (who were generally Indian nationalists), and by Akbar who practiced a policy of religious toleration. The writers of this school underscored the importance of economic disparities which was the main theme of the nationalists and Marxists. While disagreeing with the Marxists on the economic interpretation of British rule, they agreed with them in their opposition to Hindu culture. The Muslim League, which embodied Muslim communalism, was founded by Muslim Nawabs, but it made use of the strength of the Muslim masses.

The "Drain Theory" propounded by Burke and extended by Digby, Naoroji and Dutt (Dutt was the first Indian historian to point out that India's real problem was land and agriculture) was reinforced by theories of imperialism formulated by Hobson, influenced by Liberalism, and later by Lenin under Marxist ideas. While Marxist ideas inspired Indian political workers and their influence was felt in Indian political life, they emerged rather late in Indian historical writings. There was no concerted effort by Indian historians to interpret Indian history in Marxist terms. M. N. Roy, in his *India in Transition* (1922), attempted to give a Marxist interpretation of the Indian national movement. However, it is somewhat surprising that at the time of writing his book, Roy was not familiar with Marx's articles on India written seventy years earlier for the *New York Herald Tribune*. Roy disputed Lenin's thesis that India was going through a feudal system and asserted that India had already entered the capitalist arena. Yet, he argued, India was not a capitalist country, though it was advancing towards capitalism. It still had some elements of a feudal system which were rapidly disappearing. The nationalist movement as led by Mahatma Gandhi expressed the aspirations of the "distrustful" bourgeoisie. He believed that rationalism had dissolved the religious mode of thought elsewhere and it would do likewise in India. He was critical of Indian tradition and culture. His political viewpoint, though important in retrospect, does not seem to have made much impact at the time. Laski could write in 1927 that "the effort to read the problem of India in the set terms of Marxism is rather an exercise in ingenuity than a serious intellectual contribution to socialist advance", (H. Laski, *Communism*, 1927, p. 194). It was not until 1940 that a serious Marxist history was produced, by an Anglo-Indian leader of the British Communist movement. This study, *India Today*, by R. Palme Dutt, still remains the most authoritative and reliable Marxist interpretation of Indian history. [In 1926/27, Palme Dutt had published *Modern India*, denouncing the Indian bourgeoisie as counter-revolutionary and calling for the formation of a new national movement.] Shortly after his work, W.C. Smith published an excellent Marxist interpretation of Muslim communalism entitled *Modern Islam in India : A Social Analysis* (1943). Describing the transformation of the traditional Muslim community into a modern society during the British period, Smith showed that economic disparity between the Hindus and the Muslims, rigidity in Hindu social behaviour, and British policy of divide and rule were as important contributory factors to Muslim separatism as was its Islamic content. This study was banned by the British Government in India.

While there are a number of fragmentary studies, in the form of historical articles and journalistic pieces, there is really only one work, published since independence, which can be regarded as a substantial Marxist interpretation of Indian history from the earliest times to the rise of British power in India. It is D.D. Kosambi's *An Introduction to The Study of Indian History* (1956). Incidentally, Kosambi was not a professional historian; he was an eminent mathematician. Despite his intense devotion to Marxism, Kosambi regarded Marx's observations about Indian economic history as "misleading", and challenged his statement that "Indian society had no history at all......". There are other studies of lesser importance. Of these, a notable one is A.R. Desai's *Social Background of Indian Nationalism*

(1948), which was originally submitted as a Ph.D. thesis for the Bombay University. Another is S. A. Dange's *India from Primitive Communism to Slavery* (1948). Dange is an active communist leader who does not recognize that Indian history does not neatly fit into Marxist periodisation, which is essential for Marxist interpretation.

Where the Marxist, imperialist and communalist* historians converge is in their attitude towards Hindu culture which forms the bulk of India's heritage. Marxists, as did Marx himself, regard culture as bourgeois and anti-revoluntionary. (Mao's China, where traditional culture and Confucius have been systematically demolished, is a classic example of this.) Culture, therefore, had to be denounced, including religion, God and morals, as an obstacle to proletarian change. Culture in the Indian context meant mainly Hindu religion and heritage. Imperial historians, who reacted against the "drain theory" and appeared appalled at the suggestion of economic exploitation, preferred to interpret British rule as a missionary activity, characterising it as a march of superior civilization over an inferior one. Hindu culture had, therefore, to be decided and held as the cause of India's predicament. Attention had to be diverted from economic exploitation to cultural contribution. The communalists, who openly believed in religious distinctions and were naturally convinced of their own cultural superiority over that of the others, looked upon Hindu culture with disfavour. While the Marxists denounce in unmistakeable terms imperial rule and imperialist historians, they join hands with them to demolish nationalist historians, whose nationalism carried with it pride in their cultural past, and objective historians, who unlike the Marxists did not seek to employ history as an instrument of change. Marxist attacks on culture also aim at hitting at the roots and source of inspiration of nationalism, which in fact is the movement they dread most and which has effectively challenged the advance of communism in the countries of southern Asia.

---

*The Hindu communalist case is not being discussed here. They would naturally take pride in Hindu culture.

While nationalism was still young in Asia, communism had entered the political arena as a third contestant, almost immediately after the Russian Revolution. Often it took sides with nationalist forces, partly out of its evident anti-colonial character, but mainly to exploit the powerful urge for freedom for its own ideological benefits. At times, it even cooperated with colonial or communal forces, if party considerations so demanded ; for instance, with the British Government and the Muslim League during 1940s. Asian nationalism was to be the vehicle of communism, for it was Lenin's opinion that the victory of communism in the West could be speeded up by nationalist revolutions in the territories which were then dependent on European powers. He, therefore, suggested that the communist movements should unite with the nationalist movements for independence in their respective countries. Later, Stalin elaborated this theory further, but considered the nationalist movements more as revolutions in their own right, and therefore required that the nationalist revolutions should be brought under communist control and then be converted into "democratic" revolutions led by communist parties. It was during this phase that communism clashed with nationalism for the first time and since then, despite intermittent cooperation between the two, nationalism has retained its distinct personality, at times with considerable difficulty. Communist parties all over the world were asked first to fan the feelings of nationalism and then to form united fronts, the leadership of which they were required to control. The relationship between nationalism and communism remained precarious and sensitive. Communism at times mastered the nationalist upsurge, but could never fully absorb it.

Because of their constant, often clumsy, efforts to capture national leadership and their ready willingness to sacrifice national interests for extra-territorial loyalties, the communist forces repelled far more people than they attracted. They highlighted, no doubt, the problems of political as well as economic inequalities, but their fanatic belief in their doctrine led them to display a callous disregard for the wishes and aspirations of the people. They soon lost the sympathy and support of the people in southern Asia which they had managed to acquire in the initial stages. In the early twenties, they were quite powerful in Indonesia, but under the direction of international Communism they embarked on a policy of adventure, which resulted in their banishment from the main political scene for many years. Of the South-east Asian countries, only in Vietnam were they able to master the nationalist upsurge and assume the leadership of national revolution. They tried very hard in Burma and in Malaya; and they succeeded in plunging these countries into a tremendous internal struggle, almost into a state of civil war. Their challenge failed mainly because they tried to disrupt and discredit the national forces in their struggle for leadership of the masses. So long as communism worked in cooperation with nationalism it flourished, but once the clash occured, its fate was more or less sealed, for nationalism is the more powerful force of the two. Consequently, communist strategy has changed in India yet again. It is not to challenge nalionalism from the outside, but to master it subtly by cooperation, infiltration and democratic resistance. A period of indecision was followed by division among the communists. They even gave way to the supremacy of nationalist urge as illustrated by their stand on Tibet. The changed political strategy inevitably conditioned the Marxist historians, who, by their very commitment to Marxist ideology, believe in employing history to change the course of history. However, it is not always possible to distinguish Marxist political writings from their historical writings.

During the post-war period, especially since the Hungarian Revolution in 1956, there has been a tremendous proliferation of Marxism in Indian universities. Indian intellectuals also were drawn to Marxism because it appeared to be a fashionable creed, as compared with Gandhism, which was the only other alternative available and which appeared to be traditional and somewhat unmodern. The upsurge after the Hungarian Revolution was aided by the liberation of Marxist thought from Bolshevik orthodoxy and Stalinist rigidity. In the case of India, the emergence of

China also strengthened belief in Marxist ideology. As a result, a large number of English-educated Indian teachers and students were attracted to the new image of Marxism and the political activity it encouraged. The new converts visualized a new Marxist academic tradition which did not carry in the Indian mind the stigma of the 1962 betrayal. At the same time, the sympathetic attitude of the Government of India, first under Nehru and then under Mrs. Gandhi, towards Marxism and the Soviet Union, together with the expansion in university education, greatly enlarged the scope of Marxism for exerting influence. Once politics were brought into education, the world of history was also affected. Consequently, many historians became highly politicized. Some of them saw in Marxism a genuine way towards progress and others saw in Marxist —grouping possibilities of further success. The appointment of a Marxist professor led to further appointments and for those young historians who sought positions in universities, the profession of Marxism became a necessary tool for self-advancement. Thus with Marxism there developed what may be regarded as Marxist factionalism. A number of writings in the form of journalistic pieces and political articles began to appear as work of history. Political power and patronage were exercised by placing Marxists, whether open or disguised, but always reliable, in positions of academic importance, and their works were published, translated and prescribed in universities and schools. Strictly speaking, these works are not history, though they pass as such. Some of these pieces, however, are inspiring contributions, especially those which have been written by economists or economic historians. Substantial works of historical writing from a Marxist point of view are indeed very few, excluding special studies dealing with selected aspects of Indian history.

There is much in the Marxist view of history which is thought-inspiring ; economic and technological changes do determine the course of history, and class-interests do lead to class conflicts. But the sweeping generalisations and patterns which the Marxist historians draw, that all history has been a history of struggles between the dominated and the dominating classes at various stages of social development, or that history is nothing but the activity of man in pursuit of his own ends are examples of manipulation of historical facts to fit into their pre-conceived notions. They are distortions of history. While Marx visualised the force of economic factors in history, he did not realise the significance of cultural tradition and individual liberty culminating in nationalism and democracy. There are no laws in history and there is no scientific exactitude in historical development. History depends on innumerable factors, many of which are unpredictable and imponderable. Historical inevitability is a myth.

Marxist analysis of history is a worthy intellectual exercise, but Marxist penetration of the world of history is political jingoism, unworthy of academic dignity, justice and freedom.

Marxist factionalism has become so overpowering and dominant in some Indian universities that to try to present a different point of view would be to risk charges of cultural chauvinism, and anti-proletarianism. While Marxist factionalist conspiracy is permitted, the assertion of historical objectivity is not. This phenomenon is not only true of India, but of some other countries. In the U.K. a study was recently conducted under the leadership of Professor Julius Gould, which finds that British universities and polytechnics have been infiltrated by Marxists dedicated to indoctrinating students and overwhelming the liberal and pluralist values of academic life. (*The Times*, November 14, 1977.) This report has naturally given rise to an academic debate. Academics who are worried about the advent of a Marxist approach to subjects feel that it involves intellectually dishonest techniques. Others regard Marxism as an intellectual stimulant and a fertile system of thinking, which has been probably the most exciting intellectual development of the 20th century.

While Marxism, insisting, like religion, on the rigidity of interpretation of historical development according to the preconceived notions of society, fertilised the non-Marxist historian thought which admitted it as yet another mode of thinking, it sterilized Marxist historians who refused to think beyond the prescribed framework. Like the Church in the Middle Ages, Marxism has sought to use history, thereby obstructing the free flow of historical development. Since Marxist historians aim at changing history, not writing it, it is not surprising that in India today they are agitating to see certain text books retained in schools to capture young minds, rather than conducting research and raising historical controversy to a higher educational level where it can properly be thrashed out, rejected or accepted. Indoctrination of students appears to be more important to Marxist historians than advancement of knowledge.

Freedom to engage in Marxist thinking cannot be allowed to suppress freedom of thought itself, especially in India, where thought has been more free than in any other society or culture. No true history can emerge from intellectual slavery, and as Nehru said to Khrushchev in 1959, "You do not change the course of history by turning the faces of portraits on the walls." (*New york Post*, 1.4.1959.)

Reference

1. Karl Marx, "The Future Results of British Rule in India", *vide*, The *New York Daily Tribune*, 22-7-1853.

POLITY

KAUTILYAN SOCIAL IDEALS

P.C. CHUNDER

THE ARTHASASTRA of Kautilya reveals a spirit of happy moderation. Extremism in any form is generally avoided. Whether in the exercise of governmental power or in the enjoyment of sensual pleasures, Kautilya seeks to strike a middle course. Discoursing on the use of state power, Kautilya observes[1] : "Whoever imposes severe punishment becomes repulsive to the people ; while he who awards mild punishment becomes contemptible. But whoever imposes punishment as deserved becomes respectable." Applying this idea to the field of social morality, Kautilya proposes to penalise extreme addiction to sensual pleasures on the one hand and untimely abstinence or asceticism on the other. A person excessively addicted *(prasakta)* to hunting or gambling or drinking is a suspicious character in the eye of law.[2] Vices *(vyasana)* include extreme attachment *(prasanga)* for women and other pleasures.[3,4] On the contrary, marriage and copulation are sacred duties of a householder. A husband refusing to cohabit with his wife after her monthly ablution *(ritu)* commits a punishable offence.[5] Unregulated asceticism is contrary to Kautilya's policy. The law punishes escape from the burdens of the family by recourse to asceticism. One has to make an adequate provision for one's wife and children before one can take to asceticism. Even the senescent can wear the monk's robe only upon notice to the civil authorities, otherwise he is punishable.[6]

Between the two extremes of addiction and abstinence lies the middle course of Kautilya.[7]

"Be not without happiness" *(na nissukhassyat)* is his bold assertion.[8] Happiness, as contemplated by Kautilya, is not an elusive, shadowy pleasure felt by escapists from raw life. On the contrary, it comprises manifold pleasures of the senses. Kautilya enjoins one to light up the flames of desire (kamam seveta).[9] Like the traditional Brahmanical philosophers he believes in the well-known threefold objective of life, namely, spiritual *(dharma)*, economic *(artha)* and sensual *(kama)*.[10] But the pursuit of sensual pleasures should, according to Kautilya, be tempered with spiritual and economic considerations. "*Kama* is to be enjoyed without detriment to *Dharma* and *Artha*." Rather, all the different objectives should be pursued equally *(sama)* or in connection with one another *(samam va trivargamanyonyanubandham)*.[11] The concept of co-ordination of the threefold objective of life is well-known to the schools of Indian social philosophers. The term *anubandha* occurs prominently in the *Mahabharata*, Kautilya's *Arthasastra* and *Vatsyayana's Kamasutra* in connection with Trivarga. Vatsyayana mentions[12] *anubandha* to mean "the attainment of one (end) while pursuing the others" *(tesvacaryamanesvanyasyapi nispattiranubandhah)*. Kautilya elaborates the concept of *anubandha*.[13] His discourse bears a close similarity with that in the *Kamasutra*. While Kautilya discusses the topic from the angle of statecraft, Vatsyayana does so from a courtesan's point of view.[14] According to both, *Artha*, *Dharma* and *Kama* are *Artha-trivarga* and the reverse of these, *Anartha*, *Adharma* and Soka *(Dvesa)* are *Anartha-trivarga*.[15] In Kautilya's opinion, of *Artha*, *Dharma* and *Kama*, the objectives to be attained are in the order mentioned.[16] In both the works as well as in Bharata's *Natyasastra*,[17] there is schematic treatment of the permutations and combinations of the three objectives of life. Kautilya, however, holds that all-round material success *(sarvarthasiddhi)* means that kind of material success *(arthasya siddhi)* which promotes *dharma*, *artha* and *kama (dharmarthakamanubandha)* because *artha* is the root of *dharma* and leads to *kama (dharmamulatvat kamaphalatvat).*[18] The *Mahabharata* quotes Bharadvaja's view thus : "There are three objectives, three abuses and three interconnections (among them). Knowing the interconnection (*anubandham*) one should avoid the abuse (*pida*)" *(trivargastrividha pida anubandhastathaiva ca anubandham tatha jnatva pidam ca parivarjjayet.)*[19] Bhisma too elaborately discusses the inter-dependence of these objectives of life.[20] Vatsyayana conveys a similar idea.[21] According to Manu the king should be well-versed in *dharma, artha* and *kama* and, exercising his royal power, properly progress in the threefold objective *(dharmakamarthakovidam : trivargenabhivarddhate).*[22]

The implication seems to be that these three objectives should be followed in such a way that pursuit of one will automatically lead to that of the other two. For example, a lawful wedlock primarily satisfies sexual cravings but incidentally leads to spiritual merit through the birth of sons and economic gains through family life and social connections. So lawful wedlock is highly approved. On the countrary, the husband's abstinence from intercourse with his wife after her menses is discouraged as it leads to the loss of spiritual merits (*dharmavadha*)[23] probably due to the consequential failure of progeny.

Kautilya is opposed to an exclusive attachment for *dharma*, *artha* or *kama*. Too much devotion to *dharma* or *artha* is as bad as excessive addiction to sensual pleasure (*kama*). For, Kautilya cryptically observes : "If, among *dharma*, *artha* and *kama* any one is pursued excessively *(atyasevita)*, it harms not only itself but also the other two objectives."[24] In short, for Kautilya, extremism of any sort in spiritual, temporal or sensual matter is a taboo. This idea, based on the harmonious blending of the threefold objective, is reflected in many of the measures advocated in the *Arthasastra*.

In spite of this idea of inter-dependence of the three objectives of life, the ancient Indian thinkers cannot agree upon their importance *inter se*. Kautilya believes in the economic basis of all human endeavours. To Kautilya, both spiritualism and sensuality are rooted in economics *(arthamulau hi dharmakamau)* and so economics is of primary importance *(artha eva pradhana)*.[25] The Dharmasastras no doubt give *dharma* the principal place.[26] The *Kamasutra* places *Dharma* first for ordinary people, but *Artha* first for kings and *Kama* first for public women.[27] The *Mahabharata* records all the divergent views. In the great epic there is an interesting debate on the relative importance of three objectives. Vidura champions *dharma*, Arjuna asserts the claim of *artha* and Bhima advocates the importance of *kama*, but Yudhisthira supports the ideal of *Moksa* (Salvation).[28] Elsewhere Arjuna avers : "From *artha* (come) *dharma* and *kama* and, indeed, the heaven ; O King, without *artha* people's living would certainly not succeed."[29] If we do not forget that Kautilya's work is meant primarily for the rulers of the land, his special emphasis on the importance of *artha* is quite intelligible.

For his emphasis on economic considerations, Kautilya is attacked by a modern writer. "As for Kautilya, he would simply not be bothered about questions of right or wrong in affairs of state, for he boldly declares that even virtue (dharma) depends upon politico-economic power (*artha*).[30] Elsewhere he characterises this view of Kautilya as 'the sinister principle".[31] The learned critic does not appear to be impartial in his judgement. Kautilya definitely has a great concern for ethics and even in the sphere of statecraft he tries to set a high moral tone, as we shall see later. His emphasis on the material considerations of life seems to be supported by the well-known modern social philosopher Benedetto Croce, who remarks : "There is no moral life unless economic and political life is first established ; as the ancient used to say, first the 'living' and then 'good living'. On the other hand, there can be no moral life that is not both economic and political life, just as there can be no soul without a body".[32] However, we have observed from other Indian sources, that a powerful section of opinion believed *artha* to be of primary importance.

It appears that efforts were made to give effect to the theory of the regulated balanced living in the life and manners of the people. In the eyes of the Greek envoy, Megasthenes, the Indian manners and customs, however, reveals a distinct contrast. It is reported that on the one hand "the Indians all live frugally, especially in camp. They dislike a great undisciplined multitude and consequently they observe good order ...... They live, nevertheless, happily enough, being simple in their manners and frugal", and on the other hand, "In contrast to the general simplicity of their style, they love finery and ornaments . . . for they have a high regard for beauty and avail themselves of every device to improve their looks".[33] It seems strange to the Greak envoy that such a 'contrast' in manners should exist—simplicity and frugality set against finery and ornaments (and every psychologist knows that the love of physical beauty has its roots in sensuality). But this apparent 'contrast' in the manner of the Indian people can possibly be explained by a reference to the ideal of a well-balanced life.

Even Asoka the Great, who accepted the Buddhist faith, did not discard this useful social ideal. For the laity he did not preach the asceticism of the orthodox Buddhists, but emphasised those social and ethical virtues, which were more or less the common heritage of the people. It is sufficient to quote here some views of well-known authorities on the subject. "Asoka was attracted more by the ethical than the philosophical aspect of Buddhism and laid stress upon the practical benevolent activities and pious thoughts inculcated by it",[34] or elsewhere "Asoka's edicts reveal that he wanted good citizens and not recluses. He laid emphasis on a heavenly life hereafter and not on Nirvana."[35] Hopkins has ably summarised the orthodox Buddhist view on sensual pleasures : "Gratification of desire therefore only bound one the more and the way of escape was to eliminate desire of everything except of the highest good, which was to be reached eventually by absolute indifference but the way to it was found in a preliminary elimination of everything tending to postpone the desired state".[36] But Asoka was not influenced by this pessimistic outlook on the life on earth. He honoured ascetics and householders alike. Thus, in *RE.* XII we read : "King Priyadarsin, Beloved of the Gods, honours (men of) all sects, ascetics and householders and honours (them) with gift and manifold honours". Like his predecessors, Asoka strove after "comforts (*sukhayanaya)* of the people". "For with various comforts have the people been blessed both by former kings and by myself".[37] And these 'comforts' mean happiness both in this world and the other (*hitasukhena hidalokika palalokikena).*[38] Elsewhere, we also note Asoka's measures for the material welfare of all people, which more or less tally with the provisions laid down in the *Arthasastra*. Unlike the orthodox Buddhist's contempt for family, Asoka stressed devotion to parents, friends and relations, as well as slaves and servants.[39] This, according to Kautilya, is an important duty of a householder (*grihastha)* viz., 'gifts to Gods, ancestors, guests and servants' (*deva-pitratithibhrtyesu tyaga).*[40] Well-versed in the ways of human life, Asoka was fully conversant with the fact of the diverse inclinations (*chanda*) and passions (*raga*) of people. "Either they fulfl the whole or they fulfil (only) a portion (of their duty)".[41] Asoka sought to sublimate these passions by ethical precepts. But the fact remains that the royal idealist was realist enough not to ban sensual pleasures—the basis of a virtuous family life and, glorify 'the mortification of the flesh'.

The ideal of a balanced life, Kautilya believes, can be realised through discipilne (*vinaya*), self-control (*samyama*) and certain other virtues.

According to the *Arthasastra*, discipline may be natural or acquired through efforts, mainly education.[42] But education and discipline can be had only through a "victory over the organs of sense" (*indriyajaya*).[43] Control over the senses is an ethical ideal preached by various sects in India throughout the ages.[44] Kautilya also lays much emphasis on it. According to him, this victory can be achieved through 'abandoning (*tyaga*) sensual pleasures, anger, greed, vanity, haughtiness and joy'.[45] These are collectively designated as 'the group of six enemies' (*arisadvarga*) (an expression popular with many Indian moral philosophers).[46] A doubtful fragment of Megsthenes seems to confirm this traditional view : "There is war, the Brachmanes hold, in the body wherewith they are clothed, and they regard the body as being the fruitful source of wars, and as we have already shown, fight against it like soliders in battle contending against the enemy. They maintain, moreover, that all men are held in bondage, like prisoners of war, to their own innate enemies, the sensual appetites, gluttony, anger, joy, grief, longing desire and such like, while it is only the man who has triumphed over these enemies goes to God".[47] The informants of Megasthenes claim that the philosopher Dandamis is a god on earth as 'he conquered in the warfare against the body'. Kautilya repeatedly exhorts the king to control the organs of senses. In his several edicts, Asoka, too, inculcates self-control (*samyama).*[48] In *RE*. III he observes : "These (passions) viz., fierceness, cruelty, anger, pride, envy are called sinful. Let me not ruin (myself) by (these) very (passions)". The great king claims to practise what he preaches and claims that "everywhere (people) are conforming to Devanampriya's instructions in morality."[49]

It is a prescribed duty of the state to exercise its power in such a way that the subjects can follow spiritual, economic and sensual pursuits — that is to say — proper, approved pursuits.[50] So Kautilya hastens to give us an alternative connotation of *indriyajaya* viz., "directing for the purposes laid down in the Sastras (approved texts) the natural inclination of sensory organs towards their respective functions", in other words, proper attachment of the ears, nose, eyes, skin and tongue for sound, smell, sight, touch and taste respectively.[51] Unlike Vatsyayana, Kautilya does not define *kama* but his ideas concerning it may be derived from stray references. In general *kama* means sensual pleasures.[52] Vatsyayana states : "There are five organs of perception, viz., ears, touch, eyes, tongue and nose. To experience any kind of pleasure one or other of these organs should come into contact with the objects, themselves being acted upon by mind in combination with soul. The desire for securing these objects as also its fulfilment is termed *kama*. But the thing chiefly and commonly known by the word *kama* is the pleasure felt at the time of sexual intercourse between man and woman attended with other kinds of amorous sports — kissing, embracing and similar acts".[53] It is, however, the regulation and not repression, of the pleasures of the senses that is actually enjoined by Kautilya. The cravings of the flesh are to be curbed and guided by the injunctions of the approved texts, that is, proper education.

Incidentally, Kautilya is liberal in framing his syllabus for education. It includes not only the traditional, orthodox and dogmatic education, viz., the study of *Trayi*—the three Vedas with their subsidiary works, but also *Anviksiki* (science of reason), *Vartta* (economics) and *Dandaniti* (politics).[54] By his emphasis on *Anviksiki*, Kautilya seems to have intended to temper the dogmatism of the Vedas with reason. According to him, *Anviksiki* consists of Samkhya, Yoga and Lokayata. These texts challenged the Vedas on many points. Some are known to have disowned the Vedas and rebelled against their sanction. Lokayata, for instance, includes extreme hedonistic philosophy. Yet these subjects are not excluded from Kautilya's catholic course of study. "Light to all knowledge, way to all actions and shelter of all virtues is the Science of Reason ever deemed to be".[55] Kautilya's emphasis on the study of economics and politics is also significant. It seems to suggest that he is not bound by the prescriptions of religious scriptures, although he has a high regard for them. He is practical enough to conclude that the preachings of the orthodox texts might have to be modified in the light of reason, and of political and economic considerations.

This discussion was necessary to show Kautilya's attitude towards life. With all his devotion to Brahmanical faith, he is not prompted by blind orthodoxy. He takes into account the facts of life and frames rules in consonance with them. For instance, if a husband deserts his wife, Kautilya requires the latter to wait for a certain period and thereafter to take a second husband, whereas Manu stops short with 'waiting', without any provision in that context for the remarriage of the unfortunate wife.[56] However, in most of his measures relating to social, sexual, or other matters, Kautilya is in the happy company of one or the other of the well-known exponents of the orthodox Brahmanical school.

Kautilya does not share the views of the extreme hedonists who discard the belief in heaven and after-life. At several places he refers to *svarga*. He believes in the orthodox view that the performance of one's duties in this life will lead one to heaven.[57] Nor does he disown the importance of the three Vedas as Brihaspati and Usanas, two earlier writers on *arthasastra*, quoted in Kautilya's work, do.[58] "The spirit of Kautilya was, ... different. He was a believer in material joys and aspirations, yet he did not go to extremes. His ideal was a compromise or a moderate synthesis of the two extreme views of life and its aims".[59]

Kautilya's practical bias is indicated by his non-emphasis on the topic of salvation. While he stresses the threefold objective of life *(trivarga)* he hardly speaks of *moksa* as the fourth objective which is so prominent in the Dharmasastras. Kautilya only incidentally mentions that the performance of one's own duties *(svadharma)* will lead one to heaven and eternity *(anantyaya)*.[60] Manu also preaches a similar ideal and condemns the pursuit of *moksa* without previously discharging one's duties to the world.[61]

The positive aspect of Kautilya's ethics comprises the practice of certain duties. In general, Kautilya calls them *svadharma*. In the first instance, Kautilya believes in the traditional *varnasrama* dharma, which had already taken concrete shape in the Vedic age. It means the well-known division of Aryan society into four *varnas*, (classes) and of an Arya's life into four *asramas*, (stages). On this matter we quote Kautilya *in extenso* : "The rule of the three Vedas is beneficial because it lays down the respective duties of four *varnas* and four *asramas*. The special duty of a Brahmana is study, teaching, performing and acting in the performance of sacrifices, making and receiving gifts. That of a Ksatriya is study, performing sacrifice, making gifts, military profession and protection of life. That of the *Vaisya* is study, performing sacrifice, making gifts, agriculture, cattlebreeding and trade. That of the *Sudra* is serving the twiceborn, economic activities, and the profession of craftsmen and artists". Theoretically, the Aryan society is split up into four major groups on the basis of duties, but actually there are many divisions and subdivisions.

The *Arthasastra* makes a broad division of mankind between the Arya and the rest, a division comparable with 'the Greek and the Barbarians', 'the Jew and the Gentile', 'the faithful and the kafir'. The rest includes various groups like *Candalas*, *Svapakas*. *Patitas* (outcastes), *Mlecchas* and the like. Aryan society is ideally divided into the twice-born castes, viz., *Brahmanas*, *ksatriyas* and *vaisyas* on the one hand and *sudras* on the other. It is noteworthy that despite their degraded position, the *Sudras* according to Kautilya, stand within the bounds of 'Aryandom'.[62] Again, there are various 'mixed castes' (sankara) which according to the traditional theory followed by Kautilya, originated from marriages between different castes and mixed castes. Apart from the adherents to the Brahmanical faith, there are many heretical, often influential sects like the Buddhists, Ajivikas, Nirgranthas and the like. Megasthenes mentions[63] seven 'castes' viz., (i) philosophers, (ii) husbandmen, (iii) hunters and shepherds, (iv) artisans, (v) military, (vi) overseers and (vii) councillors and assessors. The Asokan edicts mention Brahmanas and Gahapatis (Vaisyas) Sramanas, Ajivikas and various sects (*pasamda*). In any event, Asoka accepts the caste system. The strict rules of endogamy, commensality or profession might not hold good in all cases, but all the ancient sources indicate that the concept of caste was, in the main, a strong reality.

No less important from the point of view of morals is the Brahmanical division of human life into four stages (*asramas*). According to Kautilya, the respective duties of different stages are as follows :—

"[The duties] of the householder are : earning his living in accordance with his own special duty, marrying into families of the same caste but not of the same *gotra*, approaching the wife during the period, worship of the gods, manes and guests, making gifts to dependents and eating what is left over (after the others have eaten).

Those of the student of the Veda are : studying the Veda, Tending the (Sacred) fires and (ceremonial) bathing, keeping the vow of living on alms only, residing till the end of his life with the preceptor or, in his absence, with the preceptor's son or with a fellow-student.

Those of the forest anchorite are : observing celebacy, sleeping on bare ground, wearing matted locks and an antelope skin, worship of the (sacred) fires and (ceremonial) bathing, worshipping the gods, manes and guests and living on forest produce (only).

Those of the wandering ascetic are : having full control over the senses, refraining from all active life, being without any possessions, giving up all attachment to wordly ties, keeping the vows of begging alms, residing not in one place and in the forest, and observing external and internal cleanliness''[64]

Mrs. Kane remarks :''The theory of *varna* dealt with man as a member of the Aryan Society and laid down what his rights, functions, privileges, responsibilities and duties were as a member of that society. It was addressed to the mass. The theory of *asramas* addressed itself to the individual. It tells him what his spiritual goal is, how he is to order his life and what preparations are required to attain that goal''.[65]

In any event, the scheme of *asramas* arranges personal ethics on a chronological basis. According to this arrangement, certain conduct is moral at some point of time in life and immoral at other points. For instance, sexual intercourse within the ambit of marriage is an essential duty for a householder, whereas sexual abstinence is compulsory for a student, a recluse and a wanderer. Likewise, the pursuit of vacations. Consequently untimely celibary or untimely abstention from fruitful work is irreligious, illegal and immoral. The *arthasastra* repeatedly calls upon the king to uphold this chronological plan. According to this scheme, *kama* and all that it stands for seems to be confined to the stage of the householder, and that too generally within the ambit of marriage, although connection out of wedlock is suffered by law in some special cases.

Apart from special duties relating to castes and stages of life, *svadharma*, according to Kautilya, includes some common virtues of universal observance. These are nonviolence, truthfulness, purity, freedom from hatred and cruelty, and forgiveness.[66] The Greek envoy also speaks of the Indian peoples' love of simplicity, frugality and truthfulness. He testifies to their 'good' sober sense. "Truth and virtue they hold alike in esteem".[67] Asoka also inculcates similar virtues. "But what does morality include?" he asks in *PE* II: "(It includes) few sins, many virtuous deeds, compassion, liberality, truthfulness (and) purity". Again in *PE*. VII he records : "For noble deeds of morality and practice of morality (consist in) this, that (morality) viz., compassion, liberality, truthfulness, purity, gentleness and goodness will thus be promoted among men". Elsewhere he extols non-violence. One is struck by the close similarity between the moral teachings of Kautilya and Asoka. The virtues inculcated by them are in a large measure chosen from the common Indian heritage, as Greek testimony also leads us to believe.

Thus, a critical study of Kautilya's Arthasastra shows how he edifies a broad principle of synthesis in life. In his philosophy of good living he tempers orthodoxy with rationalism, combines moderate enjoyment of pleasure with the pursuit of spiritualism and economic gains and supports self-control but not self-repression. Dr. N.C. Bandyopadhyaya rightly remarks : "It is difficult to designate this ethical system under any specific name, following the western thinkers on ethics and social morality. There is in it a predominance of elements of hedonism and a belief in pleasure. Next to it, there is not only an element of rationalism in it, but an altruistic tendency is also present there. Hence in Kautilya we find a fine synthesis of all these.[68]

In fine, Kautilya's view of life is not revolutionary. It is rooted deeply in the Indian traditions. The pattern of life as drawn in his *Arthasastra* resembles that of the orthodox school given in the Mahabharata and the Dharmasastras. No doubt he lays emphasis on economic considerations. This view, too, may be in line with traditional experts in the science of polity as other sources suggest.[69] His comparative lack of enthusiasm for the concept of salvation as the goal of life reveals his practical bias. In this view too he may have followed that branch of the orthodox school which lays stress upon the stage of householders and the performance of the prescribed duties in this life.

Abbreviations

Apastamba — Apastambiyadharmasutra
AS — Arthasastra of Kautilya
Baudh — Baudhayana Dharma Sutra
EHMI — Evolution of Hindu Moral Ideals by Sir Sivaswamy Aiyar
ESK. — Encyclopaedia of Sexual Knowledge
ESP. — Encyclopaedia of Sex Practice
Gautama — Gautama Dharmasutra
HCIP — History and Culture of the Indian People (Bharatiya Vidya Bhavan)
HDS — History of Dharmasastra by Mahamahopadhyaya P.V. Kane
HLC — Hindu Law and Custom (English Translation) — Jolly
IC — Indian Culture
J. — Jataka
JAOS — Journal of the American Oriental Society
JRAS. — Journal of the Royal Asiatic Society
KS. — Kamasutra of Vatsyayana
Manu — Manu Samhita
Mbh. — Mahabharata (Santi, Udyoga, etc. refer to the parvans).
MC.I. — McCrindle's Ancient India : its Invasion by Alexander the Great.
Meg. — McCrindle's Ancient India as described by Megasthenes and Arrian.
Narada — Narada Smriti
NS — Bharata's Natyasastra
PBI — Pre-Buddhist India by Ratilal Mehta
PE. — Pillar Edict of Asoka
Ram. — Ramayana
RE. — Rock Edict of Asoka
SBE. — Sacred Books of the East
SLAI. — Sexual Life in Ancient India by J.J.Meyer.
SLAG. — Sexual Life in Ancient Greece by Hans Licht

SLAR	— Sexual Life in Ancient Rome by Otto Kiefer.
SRE.	— Separate Rock Edict of Asoka
Vasistha	— Vasisthadharmasutra
Yaj.	— Yajnavalkya Smriti.

References

1. *AS.* I. 4. Cf. *Mbh*, Santi. 58. 21-22 ; 14.65-66.
2. *AS.* iv. 6.
3. *Ibid.*
4. The *Mbh.* (Santi. 140.26) recites the views of Bharadvaja, who holds a similar opinion : Drinking, gambling, women, hunting, songs and music are to be enjoyed reasonably (*yuktya seveta*), extreme attachment for them is blameworthy (*prasanga hyatra dosavan*). Manu. VII. 46 states : "If the king is extremely addicted to sensual pleasures (*kamajesu prasakta*), he will be deprived of Dharma and Artha."
5. *AS.* I. 3. ; III. 2 : The epics also mention similar views. Meyer, *SLAI.* 216-18.
6. *AS.* II. 1.
7. According to Aristotle, "Excess and deficiency are alike fatal in conduct. Excess or deficiency of gymnastic exercise is fatal to strength, excess or deficiency of meat and drink to health. Similarly in respect of courage, temperance and the other virtues, excess or deficiency is destructive, the mean or intermediate state is preservative, of the virtue" (Ethics, II. 2. summary in Carlton House Edition, p. 253). Elsewhere, "Moral virtue then is a mean state as lying between two vices, and as aiming at the mean in the emotions and actions. Hence, the difficulty of virtuous living, as it is always difficult to find the mean" (*ibid.* II. 9, p. 257).
8. *AS.* I. 7.
9. Bharadvaja, quoted in the *Mbh.* (Santi. 140. 26), also enjoins reasonable enjoyment of pleasures (*yuktya seveta*). In Santi 167 Bhima appears as the protagonist for sensual pleasures (*kama*).
10. Aristotle (*Ethics*, I. 3) too holds a somewhat parallel view. He describes lives of men as sensual, political and speculative. According to him the sensual life is chosen by slavish or brutish men.
11 *AS.* I.7 : The *Mbh.* (Santi. 167.40) recites the well-known passage : *Dharma Artha* and *Kama* are to be pursued equally ; he who is attached to one only is a contemptible person (*Dharmaratha-kamah samameva* sevya yo hykabhaktah sa naro jaghanyah". In several passages of the great epic a similar view is expressed. (Santi. 69.70 ; 123. 2-11 ; 140.57 ; etc.)
12. *KS.* Vi. 6.6.
13. *AS* IX. 7,

14. *KS.* VI. 6.
15. *AS.* IX. 7 — *KS.* VI. 6.5.
16. *AS. ibid.*
17. *NS.* XX. 72-75 : " In this connection three kinds of love to be presented through different actions are : That in relation to duty (*dharma*), that actuated by material gain (*artha*) and that actuated by passion (*kama*)". They are termed respectively as : *dharmasringara, arthasringara* and *kamsringara.*
18. *AS. ibid*
19. *Mbh.* Santi. 140.57
20. *Ibid.,* 123. 3-14
21. *KS.* 1. 2. "Man whose span of life is hundred years should divide his (life) time and pursue threefold objectives in such manner as they may be artained in harmonious combination with one another and without detriment to one another. Thus in his boyhood, reception of education and other econcmic pursuits ; in youth, erotic pursuits and in old age, religion and moksa. Or considering the uncertainty of life, one may pursue these objectives as desirable". "One should strive to do such acts as are conducive to the attainment of all the *trivarga* or any one or two of them. None of these *trivarga* should be pursued if it is likely to be injurious to the interest of the other two". (1. 2.51).
22. *Manu.* VII. 26 & 27,
23. *AS.* III. 4.
24. *AS.* I. 7.
25. *Ibid.*
26. *Ramayana,* I. 21.57-58
27. *KS.* I. 2 14-17
28. *Mbh* Santi. 167
30. B. K. Ghosh, *Hindu Ideal of Life,* p. 75.
31. *Ibid.,* p. 87.
32. B. Croce, *Politics and Morals*, p. 22.
33. *Meg.* 68-69.
34. *HCIP.* Vol. II. 75.
35. *Ibid.,* p. 385.
36. Hopkins, *Ethics of the Hindus,* p. 141.
37. *RE.* VII.
38. *SRE.* I.
39. *RE.* VII.
40. *AS.* I. 3.
41. *RE.* VII.
42. *AS.* I. 5.
43. *AS.* I. 6.
44. *Manu.* VII, *Mbh.* Santi. 275
45. *AS.* I. 6
46. *AS.* I. 6 & 7.
47. *Meg.* 122-23.
48. *RE.* VII ; XIII.

49. *RE*. XIII.
50. *AS* I. 4.
51. *AS*. I. 6.
52. *Mbh*. Vana, 33.30 defines *kama* as the pleasure in connection with touch, wealth or properties. Also verses 37.38. Sir Sivaswamy Aiyar observes : "The term *kama* is used to denote *visayanubhavajanyasuhka*, i.e. pleasures or happiness derived from contact with the external objects of sense or the source of intellectual or emotional satisfaction. The word *kama* would include not merely the pleasures of the senses, but also all pleasures derived from the exercise of the mental faculties . . . Similarly the word *kama* is often popularly used to signify the coarser pleasures of the senses and the word has attracted the same prejudice as the English word 'pleasures'. "EHMI". p. 152. Basham explains : "In its broadest sense the word *kama* means desire of every kind and its fulfilment, but like such English words as 'desire' and 'passion', it usually had a sexual connotation. Of all legitimate pleasures sexual pleasure was thought to be the best". *The wonder that was India*, p. 170.
53. *KS*. I. 2. 11-12 (Iyengar's translation).
54. *AS*. I. 2 ; Manu. (Vii. 43) and *Yaj*. I. 311 prescribe the same course of the study for a king. The practical importance of the subjects was so great that even the orthodox school had to adopt them for the ruler's education.
55. *AS*. I. 2. The great importance of *Anviksiki* is admitted even in the *Mbh*. (Santi. 318. 46-48), which states that the Vedas are to be interpreted in the light of Reason. Also *Manu*. XII. 105. But the *Ram* denounces this science (II. 100.39) and in particular the 'Loukayatika' (II. 100.38).
56. *AS*. III. 4. *Manu*. IX. 76. The commentators of Manu are puzzled over the question of the wife's duty after the period of waiting. Medhatithi refers to the remarriage on the strength of other Smritis. Kulluka following Vasistha suggests that she should rejoin her husband.
57. *AS*. I. 3. *Svadharmas svargayanatyaya ca* ; also AS. III. 7. The *Mahabharata* (Santi. 291. 13-15) refers to some views of the hedonists with disapproval. Bandyopadhyaya : *Kautilya*, p. 30, f. n. The *Ramayana*, II. 100. 38. deprecates the *Loukayatika*.
58. *AS*. I. 2.
59. Bandyopadhyaya, *op, cit.*, 31.
60. *AS*. I. 3.
61. *Manu*. VI. 35.
62. *AS*, III. 13 Also Kangle, op. cit., Part III, 144-50.
63. *Meg*. 38-41.
64. *AS*. I. 3. (R. P. Kangle's translation). Kautilya's description of the *asramas* largely tallies with that in the *Mbh*. e.g. Santi 61 ; 191 ; 192 ; 242-45 and the prinipal Dharmasastras. Jolly, *Hindu law and Custom* (Eng. translation), Chap, VI ; Kane, HDS. II(I). Ch .8,

The great epic gives us conflicting views regarding the relative importance of the *asramas inter se.* Santi. 11, 242-45 According to some, the stage of the house-holder is the best, for, on it depends the other *asramas*. The householders carry on productive activities and maintain persons in the other stages of life. In his description of asramas, Kautilya mentions householders first implying, perhaps, their special importance in society. Kautilya takes special care to keep ascetics and wanderers within proper bounds. "On the whole the tendency of most of the dharamasastra works is to glorify the status of a householder and push into the background the two *asramas* of *vanaprastha* and *sannayasa*, so much so that certain works say that these are forbidden in the Kali age". Kane. *HDS, ibid.*. 424. Thus in his special concern for the stage of a householder Kautilya does not deviate from the predominant orthodox view. Kautilya does not tell us if the asrama plan applied equally to women and sudras. We may infer it did not, although Megasthenes mentions women celibates engaged in learning.

65. HDS. II. part I, 423.
"The Oldest Upanishads speak of these *asramas* only as three types or branches of life, but not as successive stages. It is only in the late Upanishads, the Great Epic, and the Dharmasastras that the theory of successive stages of life is formulated and is developed further by the addition of the fourth stage, that of the *sannyasin*.
66. *A*S. I. 3.
67. Meg. 69.
68. Bandyopadhyaya, *Kautilya*, p. 39.
69. *Mbh*. Santi. 167, Arjuna's view ; *K*S. 1. 2. 14-17.

PRICE CONTROL AND MARKETING UNDER THE MAURYAN GOVERNMENT

BALRAM SRIVASTAVA

LONG BEFORE the modern concept of a welfare state arose Kautilya in his artha-sastra, worked out the idea in detail particularly in relation to the duties of state in the affairs of marketing and price control. Regarding the tendencies of the traders he observes that they constantly try to enhance the prices of commodities particularly by hoarding. He points out that traders unite in causing rise and fall in the value of articles and derive, some times, cent per cent profit. In such cases, traders either prevented the sale of their merchandise or dispose them off at higher prices. For all such traders Kautilya prescribes a fine of 1000 *panas*[1].

Kautilya emphasise that for all kinds of commodities the state should fix the price in such a way as to curb the tendency of the traders to make illegal profit. This idea was later endorsed by Manu and yajnavalkya[2].

As regards the general rate of profit, Kautilya recommends that the suprintendent of commerce should fix a profit of five per cent over and above the fixed price of local commodities, and ten per cent on foreign produce. A profit beyond this limit was a punishable crime[3].

A substantial amount of profit accrued from state-trading by restricting and restraining the scale of certain commodities and creating an artificial situation of demand. The traders and the superintendent of commerce regularly studied the condition of scale which was an important factor in creating profits[4]. The condition of demand and supply was another factor which determined the scope of sale and purchase of a commodity. If it was found that the merchandise was widely distributed the state adopted measures to centralise the commodities and thus created an occasion for enhancing the price[5]. Once the enhanced prices became popular, the state again found an occasion to introduce revised rates of prices, with a view to gain more profit. But such restrictions were not imposed on the commodities of daily necessity as it would have harmed the interest of the people. Kautilya therefore suggests that there should be no restriction on the time of the sale of those commodities for which there is frequent demand ; nor should they be subjected to the evil of concentration (Sankuladosa)[6].

The artha-sastra of Kautilya seems to reflect the Mauryan situation. The market was efficiently controlled by the Mauryas. Their officials, such as the Panyadhaksha and the Sansthadhyaksha, not only controlled prices but checked deception and determined the ownership of a commodity before it was sold. They also examined weights and measures. Kautilya has laid down the following injunctions for the suprintendent of commerce and of markets[7].

1. Sale of some products owned by the state (rajapanya) is to be made through one market and of centralised imports through many markets (ancka mukham)[8].

2. To regularise and control supply stocks must be controlled and licences issued to traders. (anujnatah).

3. To withhold unauthorised stock.

4. To impose restrictions on sale in favour of state-trade.

5. Not to allow the sale unless the ownership of a commodity is satisfactorily examined.

6. To examine weights and measures used by the merchants and to punish those using false weights, measures and balances (Kutatula).

7. To prevent adulteration of all kinds.

That these injunctions were put into practice is testified through his description of the fourth committee of the municipal organisation of a city by MEGASTHENES[9],

It seems that during Mauryan times there was keen competition between individual owned and state owned trade. The law of commercial distribution was not uniform and was favourable to state owned trade. We have noted above that hoarding and profiteering were crimes in the case of individual traders. But they were allowed in relation to state trading in the interest of the state.

To encourage foreign trade several concessions were granted to foreign traders by the state. They were exempted from taxes[10]. But greater care was taken by the superintendent of commerce in ascertaining the scope of export of local produce to foreign countries. As regards the export merchandise produced by the state Kautilya recommends that having ascertained the value of local produce as compared with that of foreign produce that can be obtained in barter, the superintendent should find out by calculation whether there was any margin of profit left after meeting the payment to the foreign government as taxes[11]. Next he should consider whether any local produce can profitably be bartered with foreign produce. He was also to take into account the security of routes for exporting local produce to a foreign country.

It was the duty of the government to check unfair business dealings in the market. The government punished the traders who passed bad articles as good ones. Similarly the seller was punished if he had falsely advertised that the articles belonged to a particlular locality. Adulteration, admixture and substitution for a product were considered to be criminal offences[12]. We find confirmation of these practices by Megasthenes. According to him the fifth committee of the Mauryan municipal administration took care of the sale of manufactured goods and sold separately what was new and what was old, a fine being imposed for mixing them together[13].

Strict measures were adopted to check smuggling of commodities and it was treated as an offence. Kautilya lays down that if a trader passes the toll house without paying the proper taxes he should be fined eight times the amount of the toll due from him. Even partial evasion of tax was severely punished. The sale of contraband goods of which there is a long list in the artha-sastra was also a punishable offence[14].

The above account suggests that the Mauryan Government effectively controlled prices and marketing of commodities.

References

1, *Arthashastra,* IV/2/20
2. Ibid II/16/7-8 ; Manusmriti, VIII, 401-402 Yajnavalkya, II. 251-253.
3. *Arthashastra,* IV/2/29-30.
4. Ibid, IV/2/1-2
5. Ibid, II/16/3-4
6. Ibid., II/11/9
7. Ibid., IV/2/1-16
8. Balram Srivastava, *Trade and commerce in Ancient India*. p. 268
9. McCrindle. *Ancient India as described by Megesthenes and Arrian,* p. 87.
10. *Arthashastra*. IV/16/17
11. Ibid., II/16/22
12. Ibid., IV/2/16-18
13. *Ancient India as described by Megesthenes and Arrian,* p. 86
14. Arthashastra, II/21/24-25.